New York is Now!

THE NEW WAVE OF free jazz

NEW YORK IS NOW!
THE NEW WAVE OF FREE JAZZ

PHIL FREEMAN

PHOTOS BY SUSAN O'CONNOR

THE TELEGRAPH COMPANY

BROOKLYN, NEW YORK

FIRST EDITION

DESIGN BY DANIEL SHEPELAVY

Freeman, Phil, 1971-
    New York is now : the new wave of free jazz / by Phil
Freeman ; photos by Susan O'Connor. – 1st ed.
    p. cm
    LCCN 2001088629
    ISBN 1-930606-00-1

    1. Jazz–New York (State)–New York–History and
criticism.   2. Jazz musicians–New York (State)–New
York.   I. Title.

ML3508.8.N5F74 2001   781.65'5'097471
                QBI0-700360

For Izalia

ACKNOWLEDGEMENTS:

Thanks to all the musicians and other folks who have put up with me for the past few years, as I have gone from being a naive newcomer, bubbling over with questions they'd likely answered a hundred times before, to somebody who at least gets their names right most of the time. Thanks to my editor Alexandra Zorn, as well as Jerod Gunsberg, Joanne Abrams and Daniel Shepelavy at The Telegraph Company, and Laurie Stalter, who introduced us. And thanks to all the editors of magazines, newspapers and websites who have published my articles and CD reviews, laying the foundation for this book. They knew not what they did. Finally, let me say that any mistakes (of fact or critical judgment) that a reader might find in this book are my own, and I will shoulder them proudly. Those who wish to correct me should write their own books, and I will read them.

CONTENTS

• Jason Hwang (violin)

I • WHAT HAPPENED TO ME

The Orensanz Arts Center is buried in the bowels of Manhattan. It's not as far downtown as the Knitting Factory, but far enough to make a cab ride from Penn Station dauntingly expensive. Once you arrive, you're inside one of the most extraordinarily welcoming spaces you'll ever enter, particularly for a live music performance. A former synagogue, it's got a high, vaulted ceiling which captures sound and rockets it around the space so that every note is clearly audible. The original benches have long since been removed, and replaced with make-shift rows of folding chairs.

I walked into Orensanz for the first time on May 22, 1998, to attend a Friday night, Memorial Day weekend performance by the David S. Ware Quartet, as part of the third Vision Festival. Looking back on it now, it was one of the few occasions in my life to that point when I actually believed that the music was the focus of the event, rather than the sale of beer, or T-shirts. The entire eight-day festival (it has run as long as eleven days; the 2001 program boasts thirteen days of performances) was organized, as it always is, by the performers themselves, under the aegis of Arts For Art, a group run by bassist William Parker's wife, the dancer Patricia Nicholson.

I missed most of the 1998 festival's performances. I had a straight job that kept me from catching the weeknight shows. But it was impossible to make excuses on Memorial Day weekend (what was I going to do, barbecue?), and I wandered down on that fateful Friday night intending to see the Ware quartet, and whoever was "opening for them." Such was my misunderstanding of not only the structure of the Vision Festival, but the communitarian, universalist

3

philosophies underpinning it. The names of the other performers were almost all unfamiliar to me. The Far East Side Band, for example. Who were these people? Nobody, I told myself. I'd yawn through 45 minutes or so, and then I'd see what I'd come to see, hear what I wanted to hear.

Well, the Far East Side Band turned out to be amazing. They combined the free-improv spontaneity of the other acts with a sparse Asian sound that was uniquely theirs. I could see a violin, but all the other stringed instruments they were playing were unfamiliar to me. There were also a wide variety of odd percussion devices littering the stage, but there was nothing like a traditional drum kit. The percussionist's role was a predominantly ornamental one. He never even attempted to create a primary rhythm. Instead, he offered his bandmates a series of fascinating but somehow disorienting accents. To maintain a tenuous link to jazz—and to add a steady, pulsing foundation—they had a tuba player, who huffed and puffed along like a bellows. If this was an attempt to indicate some sort of New Orleans root in their sound, though, it was either not working or it was simply lost on me.

Their music was oceanic in scope, though (aside from the tuba player) it was mostly high-pitched. It reminded me of records I'd heard by black-clad Japanese guitarist/sorcerer Keiji Haino, particularly his group Nijumu (who combine traditional Japanese folk instruments with melancholy, desolate guitar). I was also reminded of a solo percussion show Haino had given a few years earlier, playing dozens of tiny gongs and fragile tambourines in a wild, physically expressive, almost balletic manner.

The leader of the Far East Side Band is violinist Jason Kao Hwang. He led the group through three pieces. The first two induced and sustained elegant, beautiful trance states, but the third was something I'd never have anticipated. It began like its predecessors, but it culminated in a terrifyingly forceful electric violin solo, which rose out of the music and floated over the crowd like a fire-spitting dragon materialized from nothing but the power of Hwang's playing.

It reminded me of Jean-Luc Ponty's work with Frank Zappa, but far more controlled than that. This was fury channeled and restrained, not the splatter-sound of avant-rock or the cheesy heavy metal squealings of Jerry Goodman's work with the Mahavishnu Orchestra. And it was this lack of showboating, this willingness to sublimate the individual creative impulse into the greater whole, that gave the Far East Side Band's music such an overwhelming emotional resonance for me. I stood transfixed by their austerity, and the incredible beauty they had conjured out of seemingly incompatible materials. The desolate landscape of their sound, like Chinese court music, could make you want to cry as your attention was brought to micro-focus by a single detail, catapulting itself out of the thick, almost tangible quiet.

The night took an unfortunate turn for the pretentious after that. The Far East Side Band's excellent performance was followed by some art with a capital A. "New Music" vocalist Thomas Buckner performed in a trio with saxophonist Roscoe Mitchell (from the Art Ensemble Of Chicago) and pianist Borah Bergman. Mitchell and Bergman should have known better than to get involved with what was, essentially, a shuck. Buckner is, according to the program notes from that evening, a classical tenor. Presumably, he has some command over his vocal chords. But there wasn't any evidence of control onstage. All he managed to accomplish, after long stretches of whooping and carrying-on, was to send a perfectly fine piano-saxophone duet grinding onto the rocks. There was plenty of energy, but no real inspiration about the set. All I could see from the back wall of the Arts Center were three old guys, at least two of whom had decades of better work to sustain their artistic reputations, regardless of this particular evening's flailing. I fled prior to what I could sense as the inevitable collapse, and got some food from a nearby pizza place.

When I returned, the space was being "baptized" by Patricia Nicholson, who was dancing to accompaniment by Joseph Jarman (who had been part of the Art Ensemble of Chicago, but then retired to run a Buddhist dojo in Brooklyn). Once the room and the attendees had been placed into proper spiritual alignment, the David S. Ware Quartet took the stage, and commenced to explode.

Ware is a magnet for the audience's attention, always, and it's as much about his physical presence as the fact that he's blowing sounds out of his tenor saxophone that seem like they should come from a whale, or a locomotive, or an air-raid siren. He's a big guy, and he moves with slow caution because of an old leg injury. That caution grants his every move a sort of gravity—you can't help but watch with bated breath, because you know that whatever's coming, when he finally does what he's building himself up to do, will be something to see. And to hear.

He seems to want to expel something from himself through the bell of his saxophone. His tone is deep and brutal, approaching the sound of a baritone sax from a tenor horn. Free jazz is often imbued with a spiritual quality by some of its more earnest practitioners, as well as more than a few starry-eyed, credulous journalists and critics. If there's any kind of truth to this interpretation of the music, then Ware's performances are the equivalent of psychic surgery (a practice wherein a "surgeon" reaches inside the patient's body without a knife and drags their illnesses out of them in physical form). He is dragging tumors out of his soul through the medium of jazz.

Surrounding Ware on the bandstand were the members of what was, at the time, the best trio in jazz: Matthew Shipp on piano, William Parker on bass, and Susie Ibarra on drums. (Ibarra has since left the quartet to pursue her own music; the drum chair is now occupied by Guillermo Brown.) This trio had an interplay that seemed incomprehensible to me. They were somehow able to devote equal time to bolstering and cushioning Ware's rants, and continuing the musical conversation they were having amongst themselves. Like the great saxophonist Joe Henderson, Ibarra's phrases made her seem to be forever in the middle of a brilliant solo, yet she never lost the momentum of the larger piece. She had a vast array of tiny percussion instruments around her, balanced on the drumheads and resting on the floor, within easy reach, and she seemed to search constantly for new sources of small, evocative sounds. At times it's as if (and this impression solidified itself as I saw her perform on other occasions) she returns to the traditional kick-snare drum arrangement only as a last resort.

Shipp and Parker were unbelievable, interacting at a level I'd never thought possible (and which would later prove to be pretty much their standard level of achievement in performance). They emitted hundreds of ideas at once, discussing, discarding and moving forward from each one at breakneck speed, while still connecting the overall composition with threads of pure, lyrical beauty. When I'd first heard Matthew Shipp's music, I'd realized immediately that he was playing the music of my dreams—the sound I'd always wanted to hear from someone, anyone. Witnessing his performance with the Ware quartet, that impression was confirmed once and for all.

The quartet's performance was too brief. They only played for 40 or 45 minutes, due to time constraints (earlier acts had run long). They performed two pieces, a half-hour improvised sound-storm and a thick, resonant ballad, before easing to a halt, leaving a palpable void in the air where the music had been only seconds earlier. As they packed away their instruments, I dashed out of the building and caught a cab back to Penn Station for the train ride home, but I knew I'd be back again before the weekend was over. Two nights later, I watched Shipp and Parker perform as a duo, before a packed house. Observing their bone-deep interaction again, this time in extreme close-up, left me with my mouth almost literally hanging open.

Looking back on the festival a few days later, I was struck by the feeling of almost familial bonding which had greeted me. The whole thing was run more like a collaborative party than an event intended to enrich its promoters. When I'd called up to tell someone I was coming, I was put on the phone with William Parker, not some press agent. Upon my arrival, Steven Joerg of Aum Fidelity Records greeted me, and immediately introduced me to a number of other people, including trumpeter Roy Campbell, saxophonist Assif Tsahar, Matthew Shipp, and jazz critics John Farris and Steve Dollar. Everyone was glad to meet me, and willing to endure the silly questions of a neophyte, in the pursuit of common musical and cultural ground. Shipp had read my review of his album *Prism*, and while we talked about music in general, he was particularly interested in how someone like me decided to review jazz records in a death-metal magazine.

I'd attended the Vision Festival to cover it for a now-defunct zine called *Juggernaut*, which billed itself as "The Magazine of Extreme Music." To the editor and publishers, this meant death-metal, hardcore, some electronic noise, and some industrial rock— all the standard soundtracks to teen alienation. I'd only agreed to write for them with the understanding that what I considered "extreme music" was Albert Ayler and Borbetomagus, not Marilyn Manson or Slayer. I was on a mission to expose metalhead readers to free jazz, the blood-boiling skronk-n-splatter that had already been consuming my soul and my waking hours for the better part of nine years. Since high school, I'd been tiptoeing my way into an understanding of jazz in many (though nowhere near all) of its facets and nuances. By the time I started writing for *Juggernaut*, I was already beginning to suss out the two kinds of jazz I really liked. I loved the music of the mid-1950s to mid-1960s, so-called "classic" bop, particularly the Miles Davis Quintet and Lee Morgan's work with Hank Mobley, Art Blakey and many others on Blue Note. With equal devotion, though, I absorbed myself in post-1965 "free" jazz, the music spearheaded by the sonic explosion that was John Coltrane's album *Ascension*, among many other works. (There were, of course, free jazz albums before *Ascension*. This will be discussed in the next chapter. But the album, appearing when and how it did, was an unmistakable line in the sand, and merits all the special attention it has received in the 35 years since its initial emergence.)

I was also a metal fan, of course. I still am. There's a level of do-or-die commitment to the transformative power of music that's only found in the more extreme wings of rock (hardcore, heavier punk, metal, etc.), and it's mirrored in the balls-out pursuit of transcendence that fuels a lot of the more crushing free jazz recordings. Put simply, someone who's already getting off on Slayer or Bad Brains could easily be won over by the David S. Ware Quartet. So why do I feel it is important to expose punks and metalheads to jazz, particularly free jazz? Two reasons, really. The first is, of course, the egotism common to all writers. If I like something, I feel compelled to tell everyone I can about how truly great it is. The second reason, though, is more serious. Coming from punk rock, I am forever an outsider in the jazz world. Not only as a listener, but as a writer too. From my outsider's vantage point, I can clearly see that jazz needs a new audience, badly, and it isn't going to get one using the strategies jazz labels and jazz magazines have been employing since roughly the dawn of the record industry.

The problem with jazz today is this, and only this: in order to survive as a living music, jazz must reach more listeners than it does now. Which means record sales, pure and simple. The musicians, whatever type of jazz they play, realize this. It would be impossible for them to avoid seeing it.

From an aesthetic standpoint, jazz has no problems. The musicians play because they love to play, and that's a guarantee of at least occasional greatness. The only truly intractable problem is record sales. But this "profitability problem," which ought to only affect label owners and accountants, has bled through and begun to affect the way the players and composers think about the music itself. This is a situation which never fails to damage whatever kind of music it touches, and in jazz it's no different. The inability to sell records causes panic in many mainstream jazz musicians. They become obsessed with their paltry sales figures. This finance-rooted approach to their own art leads them to lunge in arbitrary directions, attempting lame crossovers and larding their albums with pop covers or special guest stars. They don't even need meetings with their labels' marketing teams to push them in these directions; they do it on their own.

Unfortunately for both the marketing guys and the hapless musicians, jazz does not need special guest stars or pop covers. Jazz needs listeners with an interest in hearing vital, engaging music that challenges on both intellectual and physical/aesthetic levels. There are many such people out in the world, particularly now. There is a wildly innovative improv- and avant-rock scene (encompassing bands from Sonic Youth to Tortoise to the Flying Luttenbachers) that is catering to their needs, from a rock standpoint, as these words hit the page. But jazz, for the most part, is not yet fully capitalizing on that audience; indeed, jazz seems barely cognizant of that audience's existence. The only people jazz is reaching right now, in 2001, are the people who read jazz magazines and/or study the music in academic surroundings. And it's safe to say that in order for jazz to move forward, or even to sustain itself, it's long past time to tell the current, rapidly aging and helplessly out-of-date "jazz establishment" to just go away, and stay gone. The music doesn't need academic listeners or stodgy patrons, from an aesthetic standpoint. Most of them don't particularly like the music anyhow. It's a lifestyle accessory, something to round out the composition of the Jaguar commercial they're living in their minds, and not a hell of a lot more.

Aside from the few avant-garde musicians who have accepted teaching positions at various points in the past few decades, jazz professors hate free jazz, as do most jazz writers. They've hated it for 35 years and they're not about to open their ears to it now. Read any review of a free jazz album in the mainstream jazz press and within two paragraphs a reference will be made to how much the album sounds exactly like what Coltrane was playing in 1965. This is, of course, patently false. But if the reviewer fancies himself a smart one (and they all do), he will offer this clichéd assessment not as his own opinion but as received wisdom or "what the jazz public believes." Thus, to an even more conservative readership, he will appear to be a forward-looking free-thinker, rather than what he really is—someone desperately clinging to the past, and fearful of genuine innovation, or music with any kind of real power. Imagine if *Rolling Stone* were the only source for reviews of rock music. Whatever was currently selling would make the cover, and the remaining feature space would be devoted entirely to the work of '60s holdover bands, whose aesthetic water-treading would be lauded to the skies. New musicians would be either ignored or denigrated, unless they sounded exactly like what the reviewers already knew they liked in established or "classic" bands. This is the current state of jazz criticism in America. The oldies act that is Wynton Marsalis, and basically every other performer under 40 on a major label, is the gold standard. Everything else is dismissed. And in true irony, free jazz performers are accused of pointlessly rehashing the past! What, then, is Marsalis doing when he records an entire album (and a piss-poor one, at that) of Thelonious Monk compositions? Try asking Marsalis' lapdog, critic Stanley Crouch, about that and he'll probably try to punch you in the face.

Clearly jazz, particularly free jazz, needs new listeners. Even the musicians themselves can't avoid seeing this. Unfortunately, they often misinterpret the meaning of this simple truth, and react inappropriately. As a result, they do more to damage their image, and the music, than they would have had they simply left things alone. Jazz musicians are not stupid people. They know they're slowly fading out of American culture, and they're (understandably) nervous about it. So the second it seems like they *might* have a toe in the door to *maybe* gain some kind of public awareness of their music, they go hog-wild with attempts to ingratiate themselves, and succeed only in appearing even less relevant than they had before. An ideal example of mainstream jazz's utterly inappropriate and embarrassing response to the slightest come-hither wink from pop America is provided by the tragic spectacle of the so-called "jazz/hip-hop crossover" movement of the early 1990s.

The whole mess began with a few rappers and producers who had a taste for bop and some of the silky jazz-funk of the early to mid-1970s. They layered samples of same into their mixes, giving the rap audience something to chew on besides the same old James Brown drum tracks. (As shocking as it seems, it is actually possible to grow tired of James Brown.) The then-peaking (in both the commercial and aesthetic senses—they were the only group who actually managed to make this gambit work) A Tribe Called Quest went so far as to hire legendary jazz bassist Ron Carter to play on their album *The Low End Theory.* But that was only the beginning.

The compilation *Jazzmatazz,* collated/curated by the rapper Guru, of Gang Starr, brought more live jazz musicians (and samples of more dead ones) into hip-hop, and this time it wasn't as successful. The songs on the album were of mixed quality at best, and a few gems couldn't outweigh the overwhelming mediocrity of the project. *Jazzmatazz Vol. 2* was even thinner. A third volume was issued in late summer 2000, but the jazz influence was almost completely gone, replaced with a wan sort of '70s-revivalist soul sound. There was also the rap group Us3, who were signed to Blue Note and had full sampling rights written into their contract, enabling them to plunder the label's entire catalog. Which they did, with some pop-chart success (one hit single, two albums).

Others who emerged during this bop boomlet were the Frenchman MC Solaar and the Japanese group United Future Organization. DJ Krush, also Japanese, incorporated jazz stylings into his music too, with somewhat more success than the others, if only because the fundamental austerity of his sonic approach spared him being lumped in with the grotesque faux-beatnik postures of, say, Digable Planets, who were truly awful and best forgotten. (Krush, in fact, grew to even greater prominence with the ascendance of "trip-hop." His latest CD, *Kakusei,* is the best work he's released since his eponymous US debut.)

The jazz/hip-hop crossover was not merely an attempt at upward mobility by rappers, though. Jazz musicians got in on the act, too. The single album which likely inspires the greatest shudders of revulsion, and the most despondent head-shaking out of this entire sorry movement, has to be Miles Davis's *Doo-Bop.* The fact that this worthless posthumous release was Miles' final statement will stand as a permanent blight on his career. Melodically static, lyrically laughable, the album is a shameful footnote to a lifetime of musical genius. Other, equally humiliating efforts dribbled into stores without even the benefit of Miles Davis' name to help them. Particularly useless were saxophonist Greg Osby's *3-D Lifestyles* and *Black Book* releases. Branford Marsalis stepped up too, with his Buckshot LeFonque project, and a solo on Public Enemy's "Fight The Power," from the *Do The Right Thing* movie soundtrack.

The jazz/hip-hop crossover was a wretched failure because of the musical timidity exhibited by both sides. This was particularly true of the jazz players, but the rappers were also guilty. In their efforts to combine the two musical styles and entice fans of each into record stores, both jazz and hip-hop were watered down until they became shadows of their former selves. None of the saxophone solos on "jazzy" rap tracks reflected the wild-ass improvisational edge of real, hardcore jazz. Similarly, the raps shoehorned onto jazz albums were routinely lame, as were the programmed beats over which the rappers urped their platitudes. Often, the rappers did nothing more than mouth empty choruses about the glory days of bebop or praise, in uninformed terms and ridiculously of-the-moment slang, the talents of whatever musician was signing the check for the session. An actual cutting contest between a freestyling rapper with genuine lyrical skills and a horn player with the balls to go all-out would have been something to hear. This was almost achieved in 1997, when the brilliant rapper Rakim formed a live band with a full horn section. Sadly, the band never recorded, and only made two television appearances, never hitting an actual concert stage. So instead, the public was left with static beats, cheesy funk-fusion keyboard lines and soulless, mind-numbing "solos" which wouldn't have been even a little bit out of place playing in a supermarket aisle or elevator somewhere.

And so it goes. Whenever jazz has tried to gain greater market share and entice new listeners, it has betrayed itself, sold itself short, and done its best to strip away the elements which make it a distinct form of music which might actually entice people to pay attention in the first place. Covering Beatles songs (an odious practice which began in the late 1960s, and continues to the present day) is not the answer. The answer is to present the music straight, and to let people hear it. Once they hear it, they will understand and come back for more. However, I must again emphasize that what works for mainstream jazz will not necessarily work for free jazz. Originating as a rebellion against the hard bop orthodoxy of the late 1950s and early 1960s, free jazz has become, over the last 35-40 years, an aesthetic unto itself. It has its own tradition, its own artistic lineage, its own totemic figures and its own future, separate from mainstream jazz and intended for different ears. Many of these figures—some who are veterans and have been playing since the 1960s, and some who have only achieved prominence in the last ten years—are based in New York, and form the core of the scene. These are, to my ear, many of the most exciting musicians working today, and they are the people whose music I have chosen to document, and analyze, in this book.

I have written this book in order to present honest information about free jazz to people who may be only passingly familiar with it, if at all. In the following chapters, I will discuss the musicians, of course. But there will also be information about the people who run independent record labels, putting this music in the hands of listeners, and the people who assemble the Vision Festival each year. I will also talk to and about others, like myself, who have chosen to spend time (which could otherwise be spent doing something more financially rewarding) documenting this music and its players. Finally, I will discuss issues relating to the actual New York scene— who's listening, who isn't, why, and how the musicians (and others) feel about that.

This is not an academic book. It is an outpouring of genuine love for free jazz and its players, and an assault on those who would demean and disparage it (and them). It is also, in many ways, a polemic. Some people are going to be really pissed off at me when they finish reading this book. My only hope is that for others, it will be informative and entertaining, and that reading it will entice those with open ears to pay attention to a form of music they may have never noticed before. A form of music which, if given enough attention, could change their lives forever. I know it's changed my life, and continues to do so every time I attend a performance or listen to a CD. The music is here. You only have to listen to it for yourself.

• Cecil Taylor

II • HISTORY, LIKE MOST THINGS, IS SUBJECTIVE

Once something (a movie, a play, a book, an album) has reached a certain level of cultural penetration, it's impossible to make any kind of objective aesthetic judgment about it. The Beatles are a perfect example. There's no point in listening to the Beatles anymore. No one can hear the records afresh, without 35 years' worth of critical plaudits echoing through their mind. Though much of their music is, in fact, disposable crap, it is impossible to disagree at this late date with the overwhelming tide of Beatle-love that soaks Western culture. *Sergeant Pepper's Lonely Hearts Club Band,* far from being any kind of timeless rock classic, couldn't be more of a '60s artifact if it had a sell-by date stamped on its cover. But this doesn't matter anymore. *Rolling Stone* and the whole Beatles nostalgia industry have had their say; debate is closed. At the same time, all subsequent music made by rock groups passes through the prism of the Beatles, to one extent or another, regardless of the comparison's validity.

The entire decade of the 1960s can be interpreted in the same way. "The Sixties" do not exist anymore. They were a temporal moment, like yesterday or one hour ago—gone forever, irretrievable. They ended on January 1, 1970. Nothing remains but the memories of those who lived then, and even those witnesses aren't absolutely sure what it is they're remembering. Age has taken its toll, as has drug damage—in some cases they may even be lying. The old joke "If you can remember the Sixties, you weren't there" is often trotted out as a way of implying that the joker was a drug-addled zombie, something which, in context, passes for hipness and reaffirms "counterculture" credibility. The shallow, infantile nature of the so-called "counterculture" is never examined anymore. The whole thing has been packaged, all its rough edges sanded away, and sold. The implication of the joke is that only those so desperately unhip as to have retained their senses would bother with accurate accountings of what happened thirty-plus years ago. Far better to market the myth, which is comforting and ego-inflating all at once.

Nevertheless, the joke is important because it speaks to the larger truth that "The Sixties"—as a shared cultural myth—are much more powerful than the 1960s as a historical era. The cultural myth of "The Sixties" is so powerful, in fact, and so overwhelming, the egocentricity of the generation that came of age during those years so all-encompassing, that our political and societal conflicts, decades later, are still framed by the rhetoric and the values of that generation. The "Sixties generation" began as indulged children, lashing out at their parents; they survive now as self-indulgent adults, insisting that the world be made not only in their image, but with their comfort and pleasure always as the primary consideration. Yet, as bourgeois as they have become, they continue to cling to the image of themselves as youthful idealists, bound by a sort of pot-fogged Manifest Destiny to improve the world for pampered suburban children everywhere. Or at least everywhere in America.

Which brings me to the problem some listeners have with understanding the pioneering free jazz records, all of which were recorded in the 1960s with the exception of a few isolated, late-1950s outbursts by Cecil Taylor and Ornette Coleman. The "free jazz movement," often referred to in the established literature of jazz history (and what a hideous phrase "the established literature of jazz history" is!) as the "New Thing," began in earnest during 1964 and 1965: Albert Ayler recorded *Spiritual Unity* and *Bells,* two of his most important works, in 1964; and, in 1965, John Coltrane recorded his album *Ascension.* They were both dead by decade's end.

The problem is a reverse image of the Beatles problem explained above. The difficulty in listening to the free jazz records of the 1960s lies, just like the Beatles, with separating the actual sounds on the records from the rhetoric of contemporary, and subsequent, critics and historians of the music. In this case, though, received opinion is almost uniformly negative. Free jazz, at the time of its original appearance, was extremely controversial. Conservative critics lambasted it relentlessly, calling it undisciplined, atonal noise music. (Arch-conservative critic Philip Larkin famously referred to John Coltrane, now recognized worldwide as one of the greatest jazz musicians to ever live, as "anti-jazz.") Even the music's defenders weren't really helpful, commonly attaching radical political rhetoric to free jazz, whether the connection was there or not. "Hip" critics loved to claim that free jazz was the war cry of the revolutionary black underclass.

It was convenient, when mounting this argument, to ignore the middle-class upbringing of most jazz musicians, not to mention things like Cecil Taylor's years of study at the New England Conservatory of Music. Critic Frank Kofsky (the white, stridently Marxist author of *Black Nationalism and the Revolution in Music* and Amiri Baraka (author of *Blues People* and *Black Music*) were two of the strongest proponents of these ideas. Tenor saxophonist Archie Shepp (whose albums *Four For Trane* and *Fire Music* are impressive, and highly recommended) joined them in their intellectual crusades. Shepp's ranting politics so infuriated Impulse! Records' house producer, Bob Thiele, that Thiele refused to work with the tenor player anymore. (Shepp once confronted a white fan who had attempted to compare the black struggle to the Holocaust by shouting back "I'm sick of you Jews and your six million dead.")

Kofsky, like so many radicals of the Sixties, attached himself like a sucker-fish to the "black cause," undermining the real work of the civil rights struggle with his nonsensical, intemperate rhetoric. Attempting to expose agendas where none existed, he asked leading—and frankly ridiculous—questions, ignoring aesthetics in favor of politics. He once asked John Coltrane's pianist, McCoy Tyner, the following question: "Malcolm X's autobiography reveals that he was a jazz lover and a close friend of many jazz musicians. Do you think this is just an accident or that there is some deeper significance about this—that this says something about the nature of jazz and the nature of Malcolm X?" The idea that one person's taste in music could reveal anything about the "nature" of that music is, of course, patently absurd. Kofsky's writing, read today, is offensive, and more than a little racist. To him, jazz musicians were a *tabula rasa*, on which he could arrange his visions of white oppression—he wrote about the music, as the Dead Kennedys' Jello Biafra would so pointedly express it years later, "cause the slums got so much soul." The transparency of Kofsky's rhetoric is evidenced by the fact that he totally abandoned jazz only a few years later. In the latter part of the 1960s, he decided that the true revolutionaries were white hippies. The Beatles, Janis Joplin, the Grateful Dead and all the other usual cultural suspects became his heroes, supplanting Coltrane, Shepp, Pharaoh Sanders *et al.*

Amiri Baraka was just as convinced as Kofsky that jazz musicians embraced radical politics. Born LeRoi Jones, and raised in a middle-class home in Newark, he became a poet on New York's beat scene during the 1950s. Over time, though, particularly following a 1960 trip to Cuba, his politics began to take over his art, and eventually rotted it from within. Baraka became notorious for his play *Dutchman,* in which a black man is teased by a seductive white woman until he explodes into a rant, which states, in part, "Bird [Charlie Parker] would've played not a note of music if he just walked up to East Sixty-Seventh Street and killed the first ten white people he saw. Not a note!" Statements like this are both ridiculous and infuriating. Ridiculous because they reveal the author's utter failure to hear what the musicians are playing; infuriating because this sort of idiocy has, through lack of refutation, become orthodoxy. Critics like Baraka and Kofsky are almost the only writers whose words remain in print, or readily available, about this music. And though they claim to defend free jazz, their work only serves to hurt it. How is it possible to hear rage, or politics of any kind, in albums with titles like *Meditations, Spiritual Unity* or *Ascension?* Of course there were jazz musicians who inserted their politics into the music. Archie Shepp did, as was mentioned above. Charles Mingus, who was not involved with the free jazz movement, dedicated his extended piece "Fables Of Faubus" to Orval Faubus, the racist governor of Arkansas. But, to paint all of free jazz with this broad brush is like claiming that X-Clan and Paris (highly political rappers from the late 1980s) were representative of all hip-hop.

This, then, is the challenge that faces the listener. To truly understand free jazz, particularly as it exists now, it is necessary to disassociate oneself from over thirty years of rhetoric. It's a difficult endeavor, because the truth is that the origin of the music, and more importantly the reason it began to exist as it did, is mysterious. The theoretical basis is fairly simple. Musicians began to rebel against the strict timekeeping and blues-based structures of traditional jazz. But why did this happen? Possibly for no other reason than this: it was time. Like the Abstract Expressionist movement in painting during the 1940s, free jazz was an attempt to break down the barriers that had grown up within the music over the years. Separately and together, these players wanted to see what else was out there. Herein, then, is a brief and selective history of important recordings, beginning in the 1960s, and extending, more or less, to the point at which this book's main narrative picks up. This chapter, and the records it discusses, will hopefully illustrate both the germination and first flowering of the music, and (in an obviously partisan and incomplete manner) its history till now.

Cecil Taylor fired the first salvos in what could be called the "free jazz revolution," as early as 1956. On his albums *Jazz Advance* and *Love For Sale,* Taylor began his career with a piano style that likely sounded (to listeners of the time) derivative of Thelonious Monk, with his use of percussive effects and jarring, seemingly wrong notes. It quickly became clear, though, that Taylor's vision was his own, rooted as much in his years of classical conservatory training as in jazz. In time, Taylor would become the preeminent free pianist. In 1960, Taylor recorded a session with John Coltrane, released as *Coltrane Time* (Warner Brothers). It was the only time the two would play together, and Coltrane was nowhere near Taylor's level of conceptual or improvisational abstraction when the tracks were laid down. It would take the saxophonist another five years to begin stretching beyond traditional notions of beauty and melody, and by then Taylor was virtually absent from the jazz scene, working as a dishwasher rather than compromise his music or record anything untrue to his vision. *Coltrane Time* is more an indication of lost opportunity than the meeting of titans it could have been, had it been recorded in 1965 or 1966, when Coltrane's style might have meshed better with Taylor's brilliant, adamant individualism.

By 1962, Taylor's style was fully developed. He would go on to refine and hone it throughout the ensuing decades. The recordings of Taylor's November 1962 performances at Copenhagen's Café Montmartre are legendary, and have been released as the double CD *Nefertiti, The Beautiful One Has Come* (Revenant). Taylor's trio at the time consisted of himself, alto saxophonist Jimmy Lyons and drummer Sunny Murray. Lyons, a more bop-rooted player than Taylor or Murray, continued playing with Taylor until his death in 1986. Murray went on to play with many great free jazz musicians, including Albert Ayler and, decades later, Charles Gayle. The music of the Café Montmartre show, though, was something unique in the musical lives of everyone involved. The compositions, almost all Taylor originals, typically began with only the most rudimentary melody. Indeed, the melodic statements could easily be mistaken for random stabs at the keyboard. Following this initial fanfare, the group would head off in separate directions, following no chord progressions, for none had been indicated. In any case, the lack of a bass player in the group removed the last thing that might have tethered the music to any kind of steady rhythm. Certainly, Taylor could not be counted on to return to a motif with any kind of regularity, and Murray's drumming was more rooted in pulses and waves than swing-based timekeeping. His style, like that of Rashied Ali, Milford Graves and others to follow, seemed to conjure the feeling of a vast ocean of percussion, a music unto itself rather than a simple beat for others to follow. Often, Lyons and Murray were locked in a furious musical debate, while Taylor went on with his own solo, seemingly ignoring the other musicians entirely.

The initial effect of this music on the ear is jarring. The listener is drawn to one instrument, then another, then the third, all the while feeling that he is missing something by focusing on one player at the expense of the others. Only after repeated listening, when the seemingly separate storms of notes have become less shocking, is it possible to hear how the three parts cohere into one solid, and beautiful, musical statement.

As Taylor's career continued, he worked with larger ensembles. On the Blue Note albums *Conquistador!* and *Unit Structures,* he recorded with a septet; as though to make up for the lack of a bassist on *Nefertiti,* on *Unit Structures* there were two. In the 1970s, arguably Taylor's most creatively fertile period, he recorded three brilliant albums: *The Cecil Taylor Unit* and *3 Phasis,* both on New World Records, and *One Too Many Salty Swift And Not Goodbye,* on hat Art. By this point, Taylor was working in radically extended form—*3 Phasis* is a single hour-long piece, divided into five sections. Similarly, *One Too Many* is a double-CD set, primarily taken up by the title track, which is over two hours long *in toto.* The group on these three albums consisted of bassist Sirone, violinist Ramsey Ameen, trumpeter Raphe Malik, Lyons on alto sax, Taylor on piano, and drummer Ronald Shannon Jackson. Jackson had previously worked with Albert Ayler, and would later join Peter Brötzmann in Last Exit, as well as leading his own electric noise-funk-jazz-metal group, the Decoding Society, throughout the 1980s. The compositions, more structured than the Café Montmartre material, resemble avant-garde classical music almost as closely as they resemble jazz. Motifs appear and disappear;

unaccompanied solos and duos share equal space with passages where the entire sextet plays together.

Taylor continues to refine his musical concept, which seems at the core of his spirit, to this day. In the 1980s, he worked quite extensively in Europe, releasing a slew of albums on the German FMP label. In 1999, he joined tenor saxophonist Dewey Redman and drummer Elvin Jones for the *Momentum Space* album (Verve), and though the record is subdued in comparison with the gale-force 1962 trio, the same ideas were clearly at work.

Alto saxophonist Ornette Coleman's early albums on Atlantic Records, beginning in 1959, are slightly less formally innovative than Taylor's records. Nevertheless, Coleman's work may be more important. His quartet (featuring Don Cherry on pocket trumpet, Charlie Haden on bass, and first Billy Higgins, then Ed Blackwell on drums) broke free of bebop without sacrificing melody. Indeed, Ornette's music is almost entirely devoted to melody. His heads on tracks like "Blues Connotation" and "Focus On Sanity" are long, discursive and complex. They function as the springboard for equally ambling solos, in which he and Cherry seem to be talking to one another, but not in the call-and-response manner of much jazz. Rather, they seem to be holding one shard of melody after another up to the light, saying "Look what I've found," then continuing on their way.

Haden was the ideal bassist for this group, coming as he did from a vocal tradition. He was raised singing with his parents' country vocal group. Haden was able on the quartet's first three albums (*The Shape Of Jazz To Come, Change Of The Century* and *This Is Our Music*) to focus on reacting continually to what Coleman and Cherry were playing, and not worry about strict timekeeping. As in early Delta blues or field hollers, Coleman's music is made up of phrases that stretch or contract to suit their emotional content. Just as Robert Johnson might elongate a particular lyric to emphasize its joy or despair, Ornette extends his solos in any direction he feels they need to go. Cherry does the same. And Haden (bolstered by Billy Higgins' free-swinging technique, or Ed Blackwell's New Orleans polyrhythms) is always right behind them, offering whatever support they may need. These three records are often cited as among the most important in all of jazz. While they certainly are, what must not be ignored is the sheer joy of the players, a joy which is utterly infectious. Listening to Ornette Coleman will make you dance around your house like a fool, grinning wildly, and that's the most important thing about his music.

It was Ornette's fourth Atlantic album, though, which gave the free jazz movement its title, and provided it with an early touchstone. The album *Free Jazz: A Collective Improvisation By The Ornette Coleman Double Quartet* appeared in 1961. For the session, the quartet was juggled around and doubled in size. One subset of the group consisted of Coleman, Cherry, bassist Scott LaFaro and Billy Higgins. The other half of the ensemble included Eric Dolphy on bass clarinet, Freddie Hubbard on trumpet, Haden, and Ed Blackwell. This octet/double-quartet recorded a 17-minute first take of "Free Jazz," then performed the 37-minute full version. The piece was sliced in half when it was transferred to vinyl, but the CD restores it to a single, seamless whole. "Free Jazz" is often compared to John Coltrane's "Ascension," since each piece is an extended work by an augmented ensemble, playing freely. However, Coleman's piece is very different from Coltrane's. "Free Jazz" never achieves wholeness. Each quartet is conducting its own dialogue, with little crossover. Though the intention may have been for the two quartets to comment on each other's ideas, this rarely happens. The effect is like listening to two records at once—interesting for a time, but overall a novelty, and little more. Nevertheless, "Free Jazz" is a vitally important leap into the void, and it's doubtful anyone but Ornette Coleman would have attempted anything like it in 1961.

Indeed, in 1961 and '62, John Coltrane was deeply involved in his relatively new quartet with pianist McCoy Tyner, bassist Jimmy Garrison and drummer Elvin Jones. They were exploring a modal approach to jazz, allowing long sections of rhythm section vamping over which Coltrane could solo until he exhausted himself (musically, and often physically as well). The music of John Coltrane, particularly that of the above-named quartet recorded between 1961 and 1965, is artistically unassailable, and includes many of the greatest recordings in all of jazz. Tenor and soprano saxophonists (Coltrane switched between both instruments) continue to labor in his shadow. But by the middle of 1965, Coltrane had begun to pay close attention to the work of younger Greenwich Village-based players, particularly Pharaoh Sanders, Archie Shepp and Albert Ayler. This interest would fundamentally alter Coltrane's music, and create a schism not only among his fans, but in jazz as a whole.

Albert Ayler's music was immediately polarizing. Just as Ornette Coleman's music had alienated as many listeners as it converted, Ayler's conception of jazz was one which invited devotion and ranting condemnation in equal measure. His music ignored virtually every development in jazz since the 1920s, returning to the turn-of-the-century sounds of marching bands and primitive gospel. His themes embraced a rough Christianity with titles like "Holy Family" and "Truth Is Marching In." Other compositions carried titles like "Ghosts" and "Witches And Devils." His first major recording was *Spiritual Unity,* on the ESP label. A trio session from 1964, it featured bassist Gary Peacock and Sunny Murray on drums. Later, Ayler would form larger groups, featuring his brother Donald on trumpet, and drummers like Beaver Harris, Milford Graves, and Ronald Shannon Jackson. Odd instruments like violin and harpsichord also found their way into Ayler's vision. The groups' typical strategy was to churn through the main theme of a piece, then Ayler or his brother would embark on a wild, screaming, totally unfettered solo. Other group members would follow suit, and eventually the ensemble would return to the theme. One writer of the time described the sound as "like a Salvation Army band on acid." Ayler's music remains forbidding and controversial to this day; you either love it, or it'll send you right out of the room. Of all his albums (and there were quite a few before his death in 1970), the most rewarding are *Spiritual*

Unity, Spirits Rejoice (ESP) and *In Greenwich Village*, a double CD of live recordings released on Impulse! after John Coltrane, impressed by Ayler's work for the tiny ESP label (which had a reputation for financially mistreating its artists), convinced Bob Thiele to sign him.

Ayler's influence, as much as the memory of "Free Jazz," is clear in Coltrane's *Ascension*. Recorded in June 1965, the roughly 40-minute piece is an overwhelming step forward, for Coltrane and jazz as a whole. Two versions of the piece were recorded, but only one was released. However, Coltrane decided soon after that the "wrong" take had been released. Impulse! quickly pressed copies of the other version, and issued them with a matrix etching identifying it as "Version II." Both takes are currently available on the CD version, for comparison.

Ascension is fascinating not only because it provides a clarion call for the free jazz movement, but because in many ways it provides a bridge between the "New Thing" and the more traditionally melodic and rhythmic jazz which had come before. After an opening statement by the entire 11-member ensemble, the piece begins a series of solos from the horns (which included—in addition to Coltrane—Archie Shepp and Pharoah Sanders on tenor saxophones, John Tchicai and Marion Brown on alto saxophones, and Freddie Hubbard and Dewey Johnson on trumpets). These solos are often fairly close to bop in their phrasing and approach; only in the ensemble playing which separates each solo does the large group seem to explode into the kind of freedom Coltrane, Ayler, and the other "New Thing" musicians espoused. *Ascension* is not a half-hearted album, but some of the players were more willing to explode, emotionally and musically, than others, and therefore an interesting dynamic permeates the entire piece. Of particular interest are the roles of Coltrane's rhythm section—Tyner, Garrison and Jones. Tyner and Jones, in Coltrane's final years, were reluctant to pursue their leader's more outward-bound aspirations. Tyner's piano solo on *Ascension* is traditionally beautiful, and Jones' rhythms, though they flirt with the free "pulse" style which was emerging at the time, never lose sight of the primary beat.

By 1966, Tyner and Jones found themselves unwilling or unable to go as far as Coltrane wished to go, and they left the group, replaced by Alice Coltrane on piano, and Rashied Ali on drums. Pharaoh Sanders also became a full group member after the *Ascension* session. This quintet went on to record *Stellar Regions* and *Live At The Village Vanguard Again,* among other albums, and took the music about as far "out" as it seemed possible to go. Among the final documents of Coltrane's musical journey is a four-CD set of Japanese live tapes from late 1966, which includes nearly hour-long versions of "Crescent" and "My Favorite Things." Also recorded shortly before Coltrane's death was *Interstellar Space,* a series of saxophone/drums duets with Rashied Ali. The album provided an incredibly intimate look inside Coltrane's musical vision, as Ali provided the surging impetus for some of the saxophonist's most powerful, introspective solos. *Interstellar Space,* though it can be tough going for a novice listener, is nevertheless one of Coltrane's most important, and beautiful, albums. Its lingering impact is clearly demonstrated by the fact that in 1999, the record was covered, in its entirety, by guitarist Nels Cline and drummer Gregg Bendian. Even with a full array of effects pedals and amplifiers at his disposal, Cline's guitar was unable to capture the brilliance and pure emotion present in Coltrane's original.

When John Coltrane died of liver cancer in 1967, jazz as a whole staggered, and seemed to take a step back. The loss of his amazing talents, coupled with the growing gravitation of college audiences to psychedelic rock, turned the rest of the decade into a fairly dim period for jazz. Aside from Charles Lloyd's and, to a lesser extent, Miles Davis' performances before rock crowds, the audience for the music began to shrink and assume the contours of the hermetic cult it is today. Avant-garde musicians suffered even more than the mainstream players, who could still get people into clubs to hear standards and bluesy blowouts. And as the 1960s dissolved into the 1970s, things became even more stratified.

The common critical consensus is that the 1970s, particularly the latter half of the decade, were the historical low point for jazz in America. Very few albums survive from that era, compared with the avalanches of material from 1950s and '60s groups, all of which have been reissued or anthologized in boxed sets. This is partly due to the short shrift given the avant-garde by most jazz historians. However, despite ever-shrinking audiences the music of the "New Thing" continued throughout the 1970s, expanding to Europe in search of new listeners and evolving artistically to astonishing levels of power and beauty. This is not the story offered in traditional histories, though. Instead, we're told about lame attempts at fusion, session work on disco albums, and other ignominious attempts by mainstream players to remain somehow culturally relevant. All that is true; but truth, as always, is much more complex than history. The jazz of the 1970s, particularly in New York, continued to be a vital and searching music (albeit of a more introspective nature). Musicians like Sam Rivers, the Art Ensemble of Chicago, Cecil Taylor and many others worked tirelessly, expanding their tonal vocabularies and creating shimmering and brilliant soundscapes for whoever was still listening. The audiences were smaller, but the scope of the artistic achievement was as grand as ever.

The 3-CD set *Wildflowers* (Knit Classics) documents one small part of this forgotten music scene. Recorded over ten days in May 1976 at Sam Rivers' Studio RivBea, this collection (originally released as five vinyl albums) contains an overwhelming amount of truly beautiful jazz performances. Saxophonists include Sam Rivers, David Murray, David S. Ware, Roscoe Mitchell, Anthony Braxton, Byard Lancaster, Oliver Lake, Jimmy Lyons, Julius Hemphill and Henry Threadgill. Drummers include Sunny Murray, Don Moye, Steve McCall, Andrew Cyrille, and Stanley Crouch (yes, the same). Bassist Fred Hopkins is practically omnipresent here.

NEW YORK IS NOW!

The music on *Wildflowers* is composed, thoughtful, and artistic in every sense. The cliché of avant-garde jazz, that it is mere formless bleating, is repeatedly disproved here. There are some long, mantra-like pieces like Roscoe Mitchell's 25-minute "Chant," which closes Disc Three. At the same time, though, there is also a nearly straight reading of "Over The Rainbow," played by David Murray and Byard Lancaster on tenor and alto saxophones respectively, with Sunny Murray on drums, Fred Hopkins on bass and Khan Jamal on vibes. The opening cut on Disc One, "Jays," is a throbbing, funky saxophone-bass-drums strut that could have served as the theme to any 1970s cop show on TV with no problem.

Wildflowers is an astonishing document. The performances are varied enough, and sequenced in such a manner, that the most palatable, groove-oriented works will draw the listener in so that he or she may appreciate the more abstract, experimental works as well. And in the absence of many other albums of the period, it's an invaluable glimpse at a whole world of music that was largely ignored at the time, and might easily be forgotten now.

The 1980s were just as fallow a time for avant-garde jazz, commercially speaking, as the 1970s had been, and in a few important respects the decade was even worse. To begin with, there was the Wynton thing. Trumpeter Wynton Marsalis erupted out of New Orleans on a tidal wave of publicity. His well-tailored suits and exciting, if hardly revelatory, playing style brought attention to jazz from a public which had been ignoring it for fifteen years or more. All this would have been fine had he been willing to take his place and play his music, and leave everyone else alone. But almost immediately, he revealed himself as the worst kind of messianic megalomaniac, delivering pronouncements with frightening regularity on what was, and was not, jazz. He was (and continues to be) aided in this by drummer-turned-critic Stanley Crouch. Crouch arrived from the West Coast riding saxophonist David Murray's coattails; he played on a few early Murray albums, and eventually secured a spot for himself as a *Village Voice* jazz critic. But he turned his back on the free jazz scene which had provided him an early home, and his writing became stridently reactionary. Where he had once gone overboard in his praise of the avant-garde, he was now regularly assaulting the music in ever more vituperative tones. When Wynton Marsalis appeared, Crouch quickly found himself incapable of critical restraint. He began writing Marsalis' liner notes, in tones so fulsome that they would be embarrassing if one ever felt for a moment that Crouch had any shame at all about his purple prose. To this day the Crouch/Marsalis assault on free jazz continues, even though the two worlds have long since become almost completely separate. Like all zealots, Crouch finds it impossible to let anything go; he will likely continue his insensate jeremiads until his final breath. Fortunately, he is taken less and less seriously as time goes on.

Someone who is taken with a great degree of seriousness, though, and whose ascent has been far more detrimental to the music than the tragicomic Crouch/Marsalis team, is John Zorn. A skilled composer and alto saxophonist, Zorn (along with an ever-expanding coterie of like-minded fellow musicians) emerged on the Lower Manhattan scene in the 1970s, and rose to cult status in the early to mid-1980s. Although Zorn had taken part in free jazz sessions in his early years, his aesthetic was always far more rooted in the anything-goes, start-from-nowhere/end-wherever improvisational style of Europeans like guitarist Derek Bailey and saxophonist Evan Parker than anything American or truly jazz-based. His composed music, particularly with his well-known—and, for a time, quite controversial—group Naked City, drew attention because of its collage-like nature. The players would leap from one instantly-identifiable sound (country & western, dub reggae, bebop) to another in seconds, creating the impression of an impatient child randomly switching radio stations, incapable of making a decision about what it wanted to hear.

This collage aesthetic betrays the fundamental problem with Zorn. He is at heart a dilettante, and this scattershot, all-things-

31

being-equal approach is disrespectful to the music he absorbs and spits back. Even his much-lauded group Masada, the "straightest" thing he's ever attempted, suffers from this inability to pick a path and go where it leads. Masada's music is a fusion of Ornette Coleman-style "free bop" and traditional Jewish music (lately Zorn has been making much of investigations into his Jewish identity, whereas in the past he seemed to be attempting to create some sort of polyglot, hydra-headed all-Americanism through his music). Even in this, supposedly the music closest to his heart, he cannot bring himself to work respectfully within a tradition. Everything he does is always diluted with something else; it's as if he's afraid to commit himself. This leeches any emotional power out of his work, leaving only a winking, postmodernist shell. He's a huckster.

All this would be fine if Zorn's fame did not actively detract from the attention paid serious jazz musicians, or if he himself were not regarded as a jazz musician by most critics. He is not a jazz musician. He follows no tradition. In fact, he undermines any tradition or style to which he turns his hand. His notoriety, and the favor with which reviewers and music journalists from the *Village Voice* to *Rolling Stone* have graced him, created an active antipathy to free jazz in New York in the late 1980s and early 1990s. The Knitting Factory, Zorn's home away from home for many years, created its "What Is Jazz?" festival (which eventually mutated—through corporate sponsorship—into the Bell Atlantic Jazz Festival) with Zorn's everything-into-the-pot aesthetic firmly in mind. Players like Matthew Shipp, who approach free jazz from a more traditional standpoint, were virtually ignored, and frozen out of even indie label contracts. Only when Shipp's self-released album *Circular Temple* was reissued on Henry Rollins' Infinite Zero label did free jazz begin to gain any kind of public profile away from the destructive umbrella of Zorn and the various artists he'd sponsored. Fortunately, *Circular Temple* in many ways opened the gateway to public awareness of free jazz, to a level the music hadn't enjoyed since the Sixties.

The rock-jazz connection became a subject of great fascination for alt-rock critics and journalists, who were eager to interview Shipp. Shipp, in turn, was eager to be interviewed, and to expose the world of music that had lain undiscovered for so long. Soon, reviews of albums by David S. Ware, William Parker, Charles Gayle, and other free jazz artists became commonplace in alternative rock magazines like *Option, Alternative Press, Magnet* and *CMJ New Music Monthly.* Gayle, Shipp and Ware once shared the lead review slot in *Rolling Stone.* Many of these magazines (particularly *Option* and *Magnet*) profiled the artists discussed in this book. For a time, free jazz got more press in rock magazines than in jazz magazines. (In terms of album reviews, this may still be true.) Today, free jazz's presence in the alternative music environment is established, and no longer surprising. As mainstream jazz casts about vainly for a young audience to replace their rapidly aging listener base, avant-garde jazz steadily gains fans. The artists in this book are the future of jazz, whether the music's self-appointed guardians and gatekeepers want to admit that or not.

• David S. Ware

III • DAVID S. WARE: SOUL SONIC FORCE

Tenor saxophonist David S. Ware is, quite simply, one of the most overpowering players in jazz. His technique goes far beyond the overblowing of Charles Gayle, or the squiggly abstractions of Test's Sabir Mateen and Daniel Carter. Ware possesses an unequaled tone, deep and resonant. Only David Murray can match his command of the tenor saxophone's lower range, and Murray is far more hit-and-miss in his material and approach. (Ware, to pick only the most egregious example, would never have agreed to appear onstage with the Grateful Dead.) Born in Plainfield, NJ in 1949, Ware grew up in Scotch Plains, playing in school bands. "In Scotch Plains," he says, "we had a very high level of concert band. The marching band couldn't march, but the concert band was top-notch." He was also hanging out in New York jazz clubs from the time he was a teenager. "I was listening to Monk, Rollins, Coltrane, Ornette Coleman, all the cats," Ware says of his youth. "I started going in clubs when I was fourteen. I got someone older to take me. Then, when I was sixteen, my parents let me go alone, and that's when I started hanging at the Village Vanguard."

Ware began his own musical career in Boston with Apogee, a trio comprised of drummer Marc Edwards and multi-instrumentalist Cooper-Moore. Apogee relocated to New York in 1973, and dissolved shortly thereafter, though the members remain friendly to this day. Edwards drummed for the David S. Ware Quartet from 1988 to 1991. Cooper-Moore continues to play solo and in *ad hoc* ensembles; for a few years, he was a member of William Parker's quartet In Order To Survive, appearing on that group's albums *Compassion Seizes Bed-Stuy* and *The Peach Orchard.*

Following the dissolution of Apogee, Ware played in a 30-piece orchestra, assembled by Cecil Taylor for a single Carnegie Hall concert, before joining Andrew Cyrille's group Maono. He can be heard on Cyrille's album *Metamusicians' Stomp* (Black Saint), and an excerpt from an extended live performance appears on the recently reissued *Wildflowers* compilation from 1976 (Knit Classics). Between 1974 and 1976, Ware played with Cyrille, eventually leaving to join Cecil Taylor's Unit, where he was reunited with Edwards. An example of Ware's ferocious 1970s sound can be heard on the Taylor album *Dark To Themselves* (Enja), which consists of a single, 62-minute piece titled "Streams And Chorus Of Seed." Ware takes a scorching solo which displays more youthful fervor than the mature introspection of his own albums. Nonetheless, he's unmistakable. Though he was only with Taylor for 18 months, Ware's individualism and fearsome technical mastery made a strong impact on the group's music.

From 1978 to 1981, Ware toured Europe intermittently, again with Andrew Cyrille's group, and then departed to join a quartet featuring drummer Beaver Harris, Cooper-Moore, and bassist Bryan Smith. The Harris albums are out of print. However, Ware's fondness for Harris' music is made clear by his inclusion of the drummer's composition "African Drums" on the *Surrendered* CD. More on that later.

Between 1982 and 1984, Ware admits he didn't work much, but in 1985 he returned to Europe, with a trio featuring bassist Peter Kowald and a rotating series of drummers, including Louis Moholo. The years after that European tour were, again, quiet ones; Ware did little but drive a New York taxicab until, after preparing himself for a major-label record deal which failed to materialize, he recorded his debut as a leader for Silkheart, a Swedish label which would soon present Charles Gayle to the world. *Passage To Music* featured Ware's trusted friends in supporting roles: William Parker on bass, and Marc Edwards on drums. Ware had known Parker since 1975 or 1976; they were both veterans of Cecil Taylor's group, like Edwards. *Passage To Music* was well received among the few people paying any kind of serious attention to free jazz in 1988, and a second album was planned. For this recording, Ware decided to add a pianist. He chose the young, and practically unknown, Matthew Shipp—primarily on William Parker's recommendation. It was immediately apparent that he'd made the right choice. Ware says his wife told him he had something great in this quartet, and to keep the band together. The rest, from the 1989 sessions which produced *Great Bliss* Volumes 1 and 2 onward, is free jazz history.

When I interviewed Ware in summer 2000, he was nonchalant about his bond with Shipp at first, saying "I was asking around for a piano player, and his name came up a couple times, so I gave him a call. We had a little rehearsal, and I could see there wouldn't be any problems, so we've been together ever since." But as our interview progressed, the depth of their relationship became clearer as Ware explained just what it had taken, on his and Shipp's parts, to get their music to the level of public acceptance it now enjoys. "He would call me every day," Ware explained. "Before this thing took off, before we had any kind of success with it, he would call every day. I mean, I knew it was Matthew when the phone rang before I even picked it up. And he was telling me, 'You know, we should get packages to this one, to that one,' every day, something, whatever. And we always used to talk. Talk it up, conjure it up. At that point it wasn't happening yet, but we used to conjure it up. And even now, Matthew's the one who calls me, since I'm not living in the City and I don't get into the stores, he's the first one to report to me when a new record review comes out, a new article, whatever, just to keep me informed with what's happening. We kind of jump-started this together, because we had that drive to accomplishment, getting things done, no bullshit, just keeping going, getting it done. You work hard enough, and eventually things will materialize, the way it did for us. We talked about this for months, and we had times where we were playing one show a year, but then things finally started dripping in, very slowly."

Ware's quartet is the best and most viscerally exciting jazz group in the country right now. Their music has evolved over the course of twelve albums. Of these, the first two were the twin *Great Bliss* volumes, on Silkheart. These were followed by *Cryptology* and *Dao* (possibly the most aggressive and most meditative of the quartet's albums, respectively), which were recorded for the indie-rock label Homestead (early home of Sonic Youth, Dinosaur Jr. and Big Black, among others). *Oblations And Blessings,* from 1995, also appeared on Silkheart. The group has released four albums (*Flight Of I, Third Ear Recitation, Earthquation* and *Godspelized*) on Japan's DIW label. *Wisdom Of Uncertainty* inaugurated the Aum Fidelity label, run by Ware's manager Steven Joerg, in 1997. And of course, *Go See The World* and *Surrendered* were released on Columbia in 1998 and 2000, making Ware and his quartet the only members of the New York free jazz scene to gain a major label record contract. (They've since returned to independence, with a new album on Aum Fidelity—again, more on that later.)

The music of the David S. Ware Quartet is unique and utterly unmistakable. It's introspective, but explosive, and nearly sanctified in its ecstatic beauty. Ware's saxophone alternately weeps and roars, bringing every aspect of jazz from blues howls to inchoate cries into his ferocious, boiling cascades of sound. Shipp hurls fist-sized chunks of melody in every direction. Parker, never less than rock-solid, plucks, thumps, and bows below, around and above Ware's saxophone. And drummer Guillermo Brown is one of the most powerful men behind the kit in any jazz group. He brings a rock-like fury to the music, reminiscent of Ronald Shannon Jackson or Funkadelic legend Jerome "Bigfoot" Brailey. Brown's power and unerring feel for the "pocket," his polyrhythmic rumbles and cymbal crashes, create a style and force almost unequaled in current jazz, avant-garde or otherwise.

Before Brown joined the quartet in 1999, the group featured drummer Susie Ibarra, whose constant search for percussive variety (through the employment of a variety of gongs, maracas and tiny bells and shakers) brought a unique melodicism to her role. The improvised journey of that incarnation of the group included the albums *Godspelized* (1996) and *Wisdom Of Uncertainty* (1997), and of course the group's 1998 Columbia debut, *Go See The World*. That disc is probably the most forceful piece of music to emerge on that label since Miles Davis' departure. A no-holds-barred introduction to his music, it arrived at the offices of mainstream jazz magazines like a note strapped to a flaming arrow. The record was free in the extreme. Though a few tracks pulsed with rudimentary melody, particularly the opening "Mikuro's Blues" and a shattering version of "The Way We Were," the majority of the album consisted of workouts in what was, by then, the time-honored Ware style: minimal, choppy thematic phrases, repeated like mantras and serving as the launching pad for epic, valve-bursting, reed-cracking solos. Behind him, Shipp, Parker and Ibarra constructed a wall of sound like nothing else in contemporary jazz. On pieces like "Lexicon" or "Estheticmetric," the trio would create minimal, exploratory music once Ware dropped away, as though they were attempting to reassemble the pieces of a house demolished by a hurricane. For the mainstream, for a major label release, *Go See The World* was an epochal, gut-wrenching record, the type of thing nobody had taken a chance on since the death of Albert Ayler in 1970.

Somewhat surprisingly for a group with such a nearly telepathic onstage interplay, the quartet only comes together for tours and recording sessions. They are not a day-to-day ensemble. This is partly due to the many side projects of Shipp and Parker, but even Brown has another group with whom he plays quite regularly. "We only rehearse now when we're making a record or when we've been off several months and we want to loosen up for a show," Ware told me. "Other than that, we don't rehearse. It's like this. You meet a person, and you both speak English. You don't say, 'Well, I'm gonna talk, and then you talk,' and like that. You both know the language so you can just have a conversation."

Ware is an intimidating presence. He's tall and powerfully built, and he looks interviewers in the eye from a head-tucked posture like a boxer's. He walks with a limp from a knee injury dating back to his cab-driving days. When he first sat down with me in 1998, he paused before answering my questions, wary of letting false impressions slip forth. In a scene built on rampant one-off sessions and performances, Ware stays to the side, only rarely appearing in any context other than that of the quartet (a solo performance at the 2000 Vision Festival, and an August 2000 reunion show with Andrew Cyrille, are the only recent exceptions). "I've always wanted to do it like that," he said, "just to have a steady band and develop my own music. I've never been interested in sitting in, checking this one out, playing someone else's music; that fulfilled itself for me with Cecil Taylor."

"I think jazz, the music, especially the avant-garde end of it, suffers from us not keeping together steady bands," he continued. "I'm interested in the evolution of the music, being thorough about what it is you're doing. You stay in one situation and you work out all the fine points, all the details of that music. I think that we [in the NYC scene] are skipping over that. There's a lot of musicians who are working here, working there, and there and there and there, and there's a lot of fine points they're not catching." It's this sense of artistic discipline that has enabled Ware to persevere through years of financial adversity. Free jazz hasn't ever made its players rich. Nevertheless, Ware has kept the quartet together for eleven years, save for the rotating drum chair (in order: Marc Edwards, Whit Dickey, Susie Ibarra, and now Guillermo Brown). His primary concern is the future—not only the next gig, or the next album, but the future of the music as a whole, how he can develop as an artist and a leader.

In our 1998 conversation, he dismissed those who might have wondered what such a volcanic band offered the staid Columbia

Jazz roster. "There are a lot of people who respect what we do and recognize the connection we have to the tradition," he said. "For us to be on Columbia with Billie Holiday and Miles, it makes perfect sense. That's where we're supposed to be. If what [reviewers are] saying about us is true, then that's where we're supposed to be." Two years later, though, with Columbia Jazz in organizational disarray, he was no longer so pleased with the label, particularly with the way it had marketed (or, more accurately, not marketed) his music. "They're just going through the motions," he said. "They're not listening to the artists, they have no rapport with the artists, they don't really seem to be interested in trying to make it better. They've got money to spend, but they're not spending it wisely. When I say that, it's just that they can spend tens of thousands of dollars, and if it's not placed correctly, what sense does it make? Speaking in terms of us, they don't get it."

This is particularly irksome in light of Ware's recent music, and the reception it has been getting from listeners. Before *Surrendered* was recorded, the quartet opened for Sonic Youth at the Hammerstein Ballroom, a performance which marked Guillermo Brown's debut. The show was universally hailed as a triumph. Ware himself looks back on it with fondness and pride. "It went really well," he says. "That, for me, confirmed this thing about us having an alternative audience. I saw it for myself, and I saw the possibilities of what it could be. We could do that every month. This is a whole ocean of people just waiting with open arms to hear something. And the only problem is getting past the promoters, to do it. Right after that show, I went into Sonic Youth's dressing room and I suggested that we do a tour together. Anywhere in the world, I don't care. Let's tour together, 'cause this works." Ware genuinely believes that if you bring the music to the people, they will respond. And more and more, he's being proven right by audiences.

And yet, somehow the respect and admiration Ware's music got from the most important people—listeners—was imperceptible to Columbia. There were many issues at work. Branford Marsalis, who had signed the quartet in his capacity as Columbia Jazz's creative director, resigned that position, and many other support staff were let go. The new regime, composed almost entirely of Legacy employees (Sony's reissue division), decided that Ware's music didn't gel with their vision of jazz's future. "They couldn't deal with the music," Ware told me. "They couldn't deal with it live, they couldn't deal with it on the recording, so we had to part ways. We were told that they listened over and over and over again to *Surrendered,* and they couldn't get it. And if they couldn't get *Surrendered,* they couldn't get it." Indeed, for of all Ware's records, *Surrendered* is by far the most immediately accessible, much more so than the more heavily-promoted *Go See The World.* One of the most fascinating aspects of the quartet's work has been its sense of, and contribution to, tradition, and the music on *Surrendered* is a perfect encapsulation of that idea. The record seems to straddle two worlds, combining the aesthetic of Ayler, Sanders and late Coltrane with the melodicism and heavy, graceful swing of Sonny Rollins.

While it's still a thousand miles from the calcified "jazz tradition" of the Lincoln Center Jazz Orchestra, the Institute For Jazz Studies or the $35-a-head jazz clubs where corporate execs politely golf-clap between wan reworkings of the standard repertoire, Ware is very conscious that there is a lineage to his art. The album's title could be taken by militant avant-gardists as a sign that Ware has capitulated to label pressures by releasing this record; the immediate impression is that it is a decidedly more "mainstream" or "casual-listener-friendly" album than anything which came before it. But it is more accurate to think of the title as Ware's artistic surrender to his own past and influences. He says he "wanted to show the relationship between this band and a lot of other stuff. There's a lot of bridges to this band. This band is a culmination of a lot of different things. An amalgamation of many different ingredients, and I wanted to show that. Another thing I wanted to do was make what we do clear. If someone is soloing, I want it to be clear. I wanted everything to be heard. When we play our collective approach [the awe-inspiring, heart-stopping sound of the entire quartet at full blast], I think so many things are happening that people miss a lot of it, because there's so much happening at the same time. So...I wanted to just simplify things so everything could be heard clearly. Exactly what the soloist is doing, exactly what this one or that one is doing."

This approach makes *Surrendered* an ideal jumping-in point for new listeners. Some earlier albums, like *Wisdom Of Uncertainty, Cryptology* or even much of *Go See The World,* were like a blast of cold water in the face, followed by a rain of boulders. The aggregate power of the quartet in full roar, at full gallop, could literally leave the listener drained by album's end. *Surrendered's* opener, "Peace Celestial," is—by contrast—one of the most beautiful ballads Ware has ever recorded. The gorgeous melody carries the listener deep inside the music almost to the point of rapture, as Ware worries away to the utter root of the piece, something that's always been a specialty of his, especially live. "Sweet Georgia Bright," "Theme Of Ages" and "Surrendered," the three pieces which follow, are more upbeat, though simultaneously even more introspective. One of the keys to the album is Guillermo Brown's drumming. Brown's powerful stroke offers an impetuousness and a drive that Ibarra (who preferred the subtle deployment of miniature percussion instruments, and a generally more abstract style) only rarely produced. When Ware and Brown go after one another, with Shipp and Parker serving only to construct a sort of boxing-ring of block-chords, the album becomes something quite extraordinary, and without Brown's efforts, this would be a very different, lesser album.

One of Ware's primary gripes is, understandably, the repeated pigeonholing of him, and his music, as a '60s holdover. He does not pretend to create his music from nothing; he is thoroughly mindful of tradition and history. But too often, it seems like his reviewers don't want to give the group credit on its own merits. The reflexive historical comparisons always remain. Even *Village Voice* jazz critic Gary Giddins, who has praised the quartet, feels he must mention Coltrane, Ayler and Rollins. Which is admittedly an impressive lineage, and Ware should be, on some level, proud of being mentioned in the same sentence as those performers. But he is 50 years old. At what point will his music be allowed to stand on its own? Fortunately, nothing makes the disjunction between critics' "it's the same old '60s stuff" platitudes and the reality of the music clearer than the trio of compositions which are the centerpieces of *Surrendered*.

"Sweet Georgia Bright," "Glorified Calypso," and "African Drums" put the late-Coltrane comparisons which have dogged Ware to rest once and for all. "Sweet Georgia Bright" is a Charles Lloyd composition. Lloyd was the one of the first, in the mid-1960s, to bring avant-garde jazz to a hippie rock audience, and Ware has spoken often in interviews of wishing to bridge that gap once more. "Glorified Calypso" is a tribute to Ware's childhood mentor, Sonny Rollins. Rollins tutored Ware as a teenager, and was the first musician to bring calypso rhythms and melodies to jazz. This piece is, if possible, even more explicit a tribute than Ware's remake of Rollins's "East Broadway Run Down" on the *Third Ear Recitation* CD ("Run Down" was, after all, Rollins' attempt to come to grips with the post-Coltrane 'New Thing,' and hardly representative of his greatest works or concepts). And on the disc's last cut, the nearly 17-minute Beaver Harris composition "African Drums," Ware does essay something which could be heard as a Coltrane style-cop. But *not* the post-1965 Coltrane of *Ascension* and *Interstellar Space,* the Coltrane against whom Ware is incessantly measured. Instead, Ware and his group conjure the modal Coltrane of *My Favorite Things* and "Afro-Blue." Guillermo Brown's churning rhythms drive Ware onward and upward, in spiraling loops of sound, until the piece at last comes to rest, and the listener exhales, knowing that this has been a journey of miracles and revelations.

Although each of these pieces is rooted somehow in jazz's past, the manner in which they are played catapults them inexorably towards the future. No one sounds like David S. Ware—unlike so many younger mainstream players, who seem virtually indistinguishable from one another, Ware's music has a kick and a raw power that makes it instantly recognizable, and utterly overpowering. It can't be ignored, or shrugged off, or left in the background. *Surrendered* is not a record of capitulation in any sense; rather, it is a record which must be surrendered *to*.

Ware understands that most jazz critics miss the point of improvised music, alternately dismissing it merely as undisciplined noise, a historical throwback, or damning it with faint praise, as though the music was a Special Olympics race where everybody gets a ribbon just for trying. "It has its own line," he said of the music in 1998. "It has its own tradition; it is its own school. The problem is, it's not an 'anything goes' type of tradition, and that's the way it's been construed. I don't think that people, writers, exactly understand what improvisation is," he told me. "See, when you go to music school, it's not taught; it's nonexistent. The creative spirit, what improvisation is, is lost. It's been lost—it's a lost art. And when I say that, it doesn't mean people are not improvising. It means that the meaning behind it is lost. Because what it really is, it's something connected with our existence. The force that has us here is an improvising power. Life itself is improvisation. All this variety you see," and here he paused to gesture around the screened porch in which we sat, displaying all the plants and flowers which surrounded us, "is improvisation. But that's been lost, that understanding. So that's why you get everything sounding the same in music, because of the way it's taught."

But again, a more serious problem lies with the jazz press, and with most writers who cover the music. When writers do bother to discuss Ware in mainstream magazines, there's no analysis of what he's actually doing. Instead, he's compared with players who are just avant-garde enough—or their publicists say they are, anyhow—to avoid upsetting the mainstream, like James Carter or David Murray. It would be difficult to imagine any players with whom Ware has less in common, musically, than these two. Murray, for all his early lip service to the legacy of Albert Ayler, seems intent on becoming an R&B honker in the tradition of King Curtis; and Carter has yet to discover anything close to an actual style, making one disposable, gimmicky album after another.

Group album reviews are also common, The *Village Voice* and *Rolling Stone* have both run three-artist reviews combining Ware with albums by Matthew Shipp and Charles Gayle. This sort of approach—having three artists on one magazine cover, or an article putting Ware and Charles Gayle together, or Giddins' piece lumping Ware together with Charles Gayle and Matthew Shipp—is disrespectful to each of the musicians involved. It would be enough to outrage any musician, and make them wonder why editors feel it necessary to throw free jazz performers together, as though it takes three of them to carry an article or hold a reader's interest. Even putting Ware, Shipp and Parker together, while understandable, is journalistically lazy. All three deserve their own space. Each has built a substantial career as a leader; each has, at any time, more than enough projects going to deserve separate treatment. There is no demonstrable need to have all three on the cover simultaneously, unless it is to dispense with each quickly and avoid having to cover them later. It shows a lack of respect, and a lack of understanding of the music, particularly given the vast differences between each player's work. Of course the relationship, both within the Quartet and outside it, exists. But there's more than enough happening with each individual musician to talk about the music itself, and give everyone their own space.

Ware is determined to dent this kind of ignorance, if not through the obstinate jazz press then by bringing his group's music to as many people as possible, playing whenever and wherever someone will have them. One of their largest recent audiences came to see the quartet open for a Cecil Taylor/Max Roach duet performance, the first such duet since 1989. The musicians gathered on the steps of Columbia University, and the audience, thousands strong, filled the lawn to hear. "I'd like to do a show like that every month," Ware said to me. "That is what is needed. The music needs that, musicians need that, that kind of bulk response. Whatever happens, we're gonna continue, but that's just correct. The music is for a lot of people, it's for large crowds of people. A crowd can absorb what we have to give it. What we have to give, we need a large crowd, I feel. Because there's so much energy and power in what we do. It's for a lot of people, it's not for a few people. It's for thousands of people at a time. It just augments everything; that type of situation augments what we do. It brings the audience along, and it makes everything you do on stage so much easier when the audience is like that. They were like a sponge. They just soaked up the whole thing."

Indeed, he is constantly intrigued by the possibilities inherent in the convergence of free jazz and rock, particularly the burgeoning crossover between the worlds of extreme hardcore, death metal, and avant-garde jazz. The idea of playing with bands like Sonic Youth, or Chicago-based death-metal/free-jazz trio the Flying Luttenbachers, or even the "metal-core" bands (Botch, the Dillinger Escape Plan, Converge) who have lately been combining jazz time signatures with hardcore fury, fits into Ware's musical universe very neatly. "It's [the free-jazz/death-metal/punk crossover] been in embryonic form for the past several years," Ware told me in 1998, "and I'd like to see it taken to another stage of development, so we can start playing the punk-rock circuit, play some small auditoriums, make it real." Two years later, with the successful Sonic Youth performance to bolster him, he held onto that idea: "I feel that we should play in other venues," he said. "We can always go into the main space at the Knitting Factory. This band needs to be heard in other situations."

Go See The World, the title of Ware's Columbia debut, is an apt description of his mindset and artistic intentions. He is far from content to languish in the impoverished circumstances the jazz mainstream seems willing to grant him. He, and his quartet, are heading out—not only with their music, but with the careers they have made through playing it. They don't care where their listeners come from, as long as they come, and that's the mindset that's going to seal their place in the future not only of jazz, but of all music. The sound of Ware's group is unmistakable, and unforgettable; now, he and his bandmates aim to make themselves impossible to ignore, as well.

• Matt Shipp

IV • MATTHEW SHIPP: SYSTEMS WITHIN SYSTEMS

Matthew Shipp is not only at the very heart of the current New York free jazz scene, he is increasingly impossible to ignore in jazz as a whole. The impact of his career on the music and the scene is undeniable and irrevocable. There's no going back to the way things were before he arrived. Shipp has changed things for audiences, players, record companies and the jazz press.

A tall, skinny 40-year-old, Shipp gazes out from behind small, wire-rimmed glasses. He speaks in a soft, rumbling voice, laughing a lot. His speech patterns are, like his piano playing, a furious and constant flow of ideas. Unlike his music, which rarely if ever seems random or confused, when speaking he often gets ahead of himself or heads off on a tangent, and has to double back and rediscover the main thrust of where he was going to begin with. But, just as his albums and performances all emanate from an all-encompassing musical concept, Shipp's conversation is always centered on one idea—music. Playing it, selling the records, and getting people to listen. Other topics come up—boxing, professional wrestling, *Buffy The Vampire Slayer*—but Shipp is always ready to talk business.

Shipp keeps close tabs on the music scene, particularly in New York. He knows at all times who is writing about the music, and what they're saying. Almost every day, he makes the rounds of lower Manhattan record stores, checking on which of the twenty or so CDs he's recorded as a leader are selling. (When his recordings with the David S. Ware Quartet, Roscoe Mitchell's Note Factory, Other

Dimensions In Music, Brazilian saxophonist Ivo Perelman and others are factored in, Shipp's discography nearly doubles.) He's virtually a fixture at Kim's, Other Music and Tower Records, all of which are neighborhood stores for the longtime Lower East Side resident.

Over the past decade, Shipp's popularity and public profile have steadily grown. His name appears in the jazz press even more than David Ware's or William Parker's (though Parker and Shipp are often mentioned in the same sentence, as they are creative partners on the deepest level). Shipp is well-known in New York, particularly among underground music fans with little or no connection to the rest of the jazz scene. "We are college radio, when it comes to jazz," Shipp says, as an example. "Or when you have coming into existence stores like Kim's or Other Music that have a very small jazz section, but who do they have? They have me, David Ware...there's no Wynton [Marsalis]. At Other Music, there's no Miles Davis, but we're the jazz section. And across the country, there's mom-and-pop stores that have that ethos, and we're there."

Initially, Shipp emerged as part of the weird cross-pollination between the worlds of indie rock and punk and the initially insular New York free jazz scene. Until almost the middle of the 1990s, the few people playing free jazz were not only outcasts from mainstream jazz, they were virtually ignored even by the underground or avant-garde scene of the day. When Shipp moved to New York in 1984, the stratification of the City's musical environment was immediately apparent. "The only things that were happening were they Wynton thing—the 'neo-conservative' thing— and the white avant-gardists that were downtown, the whole Zorn, post-Zorn thing," he explains. "And for a black musician to be trying to actually play an instrument in their own style—people didn't even listen to the content. All they heard is that you were sitting there improvising, so they think of you [as being] in the Cecil Taylor school. To actually listen and see that you're actually playing different ideas didn't even occur to them, so they just write you off. So I entered a political environment where there was just no place for me. The Howard Mandels [*Down Beat* writer and author of *Future Jazz* (Oxford University Press 1999)] and all those people kinda wrote me off and laughed at me. The only white critic of that school who actually paid attention to me was Gene Santoro of the *Daily News*."

Shipp's music has been embraced by the alternative rock community, causing a significant change in the perception of free jazz, due in large part to his *de facto* sponsorship by punk-rock figurehead Henry Rollins, who reissued two of Shipp's albums (*Circular Temple* and *Zo*) on his Infinite Zero label. Rollins also released three albums of new material (*2-Z, Flow Of X,* and *Critical Mass*) on his other label, 2.13.61, becoming Shipp's patron and ambassador to the rock world. Shipp is very much aware that without Rollins' support, his career would likely not be where it is today. "It [the indie-rock crossover] was perfect for me," he says, "because I fit right into the ethos of Henry and those people, because the music was the most vital thing. It was a home. And it was a home with people with profile, so the little jazz ghetto, instantly I was a notch above them just by virtue of being with people with an actual name in American culture really feeling something with your music. So it put me on a level above the little ghettoized critics that wouldn't give me the time of day before. I instantly, in a second, was above them." The fact that it's no longer in any way shocking to see a free jazz album reviewed in *CMJ, Alternative Press* or *Magnet* is a tribute to the change in public perception created by Shipp's and Rollins' efforts. "It's not still alive in the sense that it was then, with the whole surprise element, 'Wow! Alternative rock kids are listening to jazz!'" Shipp says. "That's over, that initial wave, but it did give us a foothold in the marketplace in a lot of ways."

Shipp's debut album is *Sonic Explorations* (Cadence), a duo with alto saxophonist Rob Brown. But it was *Circular Temple,* a trio session with William Parker and drummer Whit Dickey, which launched him into the public eye. Like many of his other records (*Strata,*

Thesis, Zo, Prism) it is a suite in multiple parts. The four sections of *Circular Temple* are thematically similar, but stylistically very different from one another. In particular, "Circular Temple #2 (Monk's Nightmare)" stands out from the other three. As its title would indicate, it is the most bop-rooted section of the album, but as John Farris wrote in the liner notes, "Monk would have been transfixed, terrified." The cut begins with a relatively simple, straight-ahead melodic figure, actually more similar to Bud Powell than Thelonious Monk. Soon, though, Shipp begins breaking the melody into chunks, and heads decisively towards the lower range of the keyboard. His piano rumbles along beside William Parker's bass for long moments, the two creating a percussive, angular duet. Whit Dickey's flat, dry drumming complements the pair's work brilliantly, but as with all Shipp/Parker recordings, the duo interaction is paramount. Over the course of the piece's ten-minute running time, Shipp returns often to beautiful, melodic figures, but the overall tone is one of great abstraction, and the music is often more violent than his later work. In these early recordings, it is easy to see how a listener might make the connection with Cecil Taylor's trio recordings, particularly works from the 1980s, which feature Parker on bass.

The Taylor comparison was natural early in Shipp's career. Yet, even after it ceased to be in any way applicable, it dogged him for years. It occasionally still shows up, but for the most part Shipp's own notoriety forces all but the most obstinate critics to hear his music on its own merits. Actually sitting down and listening to the two players today reveals obvious differences in their respective styles, particularly as Shipp's music has evolved to its present remarkable levels.

Obviously, without Taylor's pioneering work, no one would have had any reference point for Shipp's aesthetic when he appeared. And indeed, he has cited Taylor as a strong formative influence. At this point, though, there is relatively little which connects Shipp's music to Taylor's. Where Taylor quite often still concentrates on percussive effects, to the detriment of melody, Shipp tends to focus more and more on the melody of a piece, pulling it apart bit by bit, until only the tiniest shreds remain, then carefully reassembling it. Shipp's compositions and performances are circular in nature—there is always a clear progression from start to finish, and back to the start again. Taylor's pieces, by contrast, seem like one-way journeys. On occasion, Taylor's compositions fail to achieve forward motion at all, and give the impression of treading water.

More interestingly, for all of Taylor's concern with creating percussive sounds on the keyboard, hammering the keys with such force it seems like they'll fly off, Shipp's music is much more rhythmic. Taylor's pieces are often quite arrhythmic; although he has worked with many of jazz's greatest drummers (Sunny Murray, Ronald Shannon Jackson, Kenny Clarke, Max Roach), they often seem to be battling with him, attempting to force him back into line. Shipp, on the other hand, very much embraces rhythmic interplay. This is particularly obvious in his recordings with the David S. Ware Quartet and its drummers Whit Dickey and Guillermo Brown. Even when there is no drummer present, though, as on *Zo* and *DNA* (both duo albums with William Parker), *Thesis* (a duo with guitarist Joe Morris), or *Strata* (a record by Shipp's "Horn Quartet": trumpeter Roy Campbell, saxophonist Daniel Carter, and Parker on bass), Shipp's playing often centers on rhythm. A definite forward impetus is always present. *DNA* in particular is an intensely rhythmic album, with compositions like the title track and a throbbing version of "When Johnny Comes Marching Home" dragging the listener along like a commuter with his arm caught in a subway door. This is where Shipp's other major influences, Thelonious Monk and Bud Powell, are most clearly evident.

Aside from the comparisons to Taylor, the other baffling thing for Shipp is the persistent criticism that free jazz is somehow purely emotional and turbulent, without the intellectual underpinning of bop and post-bop styles. "I think this music is open to all kinds of misunderstandings," he says charitably. "Even somebody like Albert Ayler, if you really listen to his playing, it's very well thought-out,

NEW YORK IS NOW!

and actually quite intellectual. It's a complete system. If you listen to him just playing off the horn, and then you listen to other people doing it, you realize that the reason he's an icon is because he really had a system. There's a real intellect behind his improvising. That's obviously the case with Cecil Taylor [as well]. I mean, if somebody has longevity as an artist, it definitely means there's thought behind their work. They're not getting up there just jacking off...'Look at me, I've got these deep feelings and I'm expressing myself.' I mean, maybe part of the appeal is that [the player] is wearing his feelings on his sleeve, but that has to be translated into some kind of system or body of work that has some type of logic and therefore makes sense over a series of CDs. I don't understand that [free jazz as emotional versus intellectual music] sentiment, and I think it's a disservice to various practitioners of that art. And also, if you're going to point to what makes all of their music different, the whole Apollonian versus Dionysian [dichotomy], there's an Apollonian element in each one that makes their Dionysian frenzies different. So you know why Albert Ayler's body of work is different from Sun Ra's or Coltrane's. Even if they are all dealing in that emotional pool or whatever, there's still definitely some guiding intelligence behind all their work that allows it to continue to exist on CDs and sell because people are still interested in it, and identify it [as well], because if it was all Dionysian it would just all sound the same. I think that whole way of looking at jazz is tired, and has absolutely nothing to do with someone like myself."

Surprisingly, this misinterpretation of the music seems primarily confined to jazz critics. Rock listeners, according to Shipp, grasp the music much more quickly, in all its depth. "I think," he says, "that the people that got into us, it wasn't like they were just 'Oh wow, free jazz, noisy...' No, it really spawned a whole new generation of really bright people who could really identify what they actually liked about the music. So it wasn't just a matter of not liking certain types of rock bands, 'cause they're too poppish, so we're looking for something experimental. The people that came to us can really identify the melodic aspects of what we do that they like, and I've seen a lot of cases where people came to us first and they gave themselves a real education in jazz history really quickly, and they kind of grasped the whole thing. And that's why when you look at *Down Beat* [May 2000 issue] I'm one of the main features. My picture is in the table of contents. Or you look at *Jazziz* and William's on the cover. The jazz world has begrudgingly, even though they're condescending, had to acknowledge that we've really brought a lot of people into jazz and they're not idiots. Because the people that tend to get into us," and here he begins to laugh, "and I'm really patting ourselves on the back here, a lot of them tend to be brighter than the people who are just into jazz, who are some stupid motherfuckers."

Shipp has little patience with the jazz press. "You can pretty much every year predict at least six of the covers. Pat Metheny'll be on one, Michael Brecker'll be on, Wynton, David Sanborn...I mean, it's a joke." He continues, "I know for a fact that those magazines don't even sell albums. I track five-star reviews all around town, and I've seen five-star, lead review albums in *Down Beat* not sell one album in New York that month. So what does that say? I don't know who could possibly take those magazines seriously." Even as he blasts many members of the jazz press, though (lampooning one relatively well-known critic and author in particular, who according to Shipp "hates me, like a truly passionate hatred. [But] he's been pushed into writing about me because he's a complete mercenary as a writer"), he claims to see their side; understanding, for example, why free jazz is labeled a '60s holdover while musicians still playing the bop changes of the 1950s are given a pass. "I think the logic in a critic's mind is that at least that music can be said to be functional. Like, if they're writing for a newspaper, for a daily, you tell people this is pleasant, you could go out to a club, take your date or whatever. And our music, since it's not functional in that sense, they feel a license to dig and get lazy...where some young player on Blue Note...I mean, what are they gonna say? I don't even subscribe to the idea that everybody should be an innovator. I mean, if somebody likes to play like Bill Evans and they do it well then more power to them. I don't want to hear it, but maybe somebody does."

Some would find it surprising that for all his success in bringing free jazz to new audiences, Shipp has never been seriously approached by any of the major record labels. "There's been word out that people have been paying attention to my career," he says, "honchos from majors who have expressed admiration, but as far as going past that, no. There's been word at certain points in my career that somebody was trying to push me on [major labels], and that they actually knew of me, liked me, and then I've met people and there's been lip service paid to my body of work." Is it because, as with rock bands, they want him to achieve a certain level of sales before scooping him up and trumpeting him as their latest "discovery"? Shipp has his doubts. "I don't even know if it's a matter of getting further in my career. Because the thing with Branford [Marsalis] and David [Ware], I mean, I remember the concert in France where he [Marsalis] heard us, and it was years before he got the job [Creative Director of Columbia Jazz—since resigned], but he came backstage and his mouth was watering then. And when he got in a position of power, he wanted to shake things up there. So it's always a question of somebody who has the will to shake things up, and actually likes the music, gets into a position of power to do it. But I don't think it's a waiting thing. I think they're too stupid to see that this period's going to make sense 20 years from now. I think most of the people at major labels are too stupid to see it. I also think that the whole major label jazz thing is crumbling anyway, completely eroding. It has no center, no vision, no life, no nothing. So I don't really wanna be there. To me it doesn't really have any relevance. The only thing that matters is that you will be in every bin in every little store, but what does that matter if there's no vision or will to present you properly to the public? You can sell maybe a thousand more albums, because there's 20,000 more shipped. So you sell a thousand more albums in the short term, or maybe you get a bigger cash advance.

But I'm building my career at a very slow pace with a very organic logic, and I'm very happy to be doing it that way, the way it's unfolding."

Over the past few years, Shipp has released records through three primary sources. His contract with Rollins' 2.13.61 label yielded three albums—*2-Z* (a duo with Art Ensemble of Chicago founder Roscoe Mitchell), *Flow Of X* and *Critical Mass*. He released several albums, including *By The Law Of Music, The Multiplication Table, Thesis, Strata,* and *Gravitational Systems,* through the Swiss label hat Art. And most recently, he has released *DNA, Pastoral Composure* and *New Orbit* for the New York indie-rock label Thirsty Ear. Over the years, of course, other albums have emerged on labels like Silkheart, No More Records, Cadence Jazz, and the famed German label FMP (Free Music Productions), which has released work by Cecil Taylor, Peter Brotzmann, and many other performers. One of his most interesting albums, originally released on Brinkmann Records but now reissued by hat Art, is 1993's *Prism. Prism* is a live trio set from the lower Manhattan performance space Roulette, featuring the trio of Shipp, Parker, and Dickey. Running roughly an hour, it consists of two pieces, titled (in typical fashion) "Prism I" and "Prism II."

Beginning with a simple, seesawing melody, "Prism I" quickly explodes into an almost swinging mode, Whit Dickey's ride cymbal and sidelong drum accents sending the trio careening forwards. Shipp keeps the piece from being entirely overtaken by sheer forward momentum, by continuing to break the melody into small, jagged shards. Parker and Dickey seem to be working on him, though, and influencing him, and soon he is creating long streams of low-end rumbles, great washes of notes which engulf the listener and make it impossible to do anything else but focus on the music, to hear where it's going to go next. "Prism II," like the second half of John Coltrane's *Meditations,* begins softly, with Shipp playing solo. He explores gently and carefully for a few moments, finding his way. When Dickey and Parker come in again, about four minutes into the piece, the momentum is again overwhelming and sudden. *Prism* is not an album commonly cited as one of Shipp's career landmarks, but it should be. It deserves much more attention than it has received to date.

One advantage to working with multiple record labels has been that Shipp's experimentalism has been allowed to flower. He changes the lineup of musicians, and the instrumentation, with virtually every album. He returns, naturally, to core groups, but never releases three piano trio records in a row, for example. The trio with Parker and Dickey appears on *Circular Temple, Prism, Points, Flow Of X* and *Critical Mass.* On *Points* Rob Brown plays alto saxophone, and on *Flow Of X* and *Critical Mass* the trio is joined by violinist Mat Maneri. Shipp also uses Maneri in his "String Trio" (piano, bass and violin) on *By The Law Of Music,* and duets with him on *Gravitational Systems. Zo* and *DNA* are duos with Parker, *Sonic Explorations* is a duo with Brown, and *Thesis* is a duo with guitarist Joe Morris. On *The Multiplication Table,* Susie Ibarra replaces Whit Dickey as drummer. Ibarra was, at the time, also drumming for the David S. Ware Quartet. On *Pastoral Composure,* Shipp and Parker are joined by Roy Campbell on trumpet, and Gerald Cleaver on drums. Perhaps the most unique lineup, though, appears on 1998's *Strata* (hat Art).

Shipp has long admired the work of the fully-improvisational quartet Other Dimensions In Music. A group featuring Roy Campbell, William Parker, saxophonist Daniel Carter and drummer Rashid Bakr, ODIM has been together for nearly twenty years. During that time they have recorded only three albums; a self-titled 1988 debut for Silkheart, and two releases on Aum Fidelity—1997's *Now!* and 1999's *Time Is Of The Essence; The Essence Is Beyond Time,* a live recording which featured Shipp as a guest. For *Strata,* Shipp brought in all the members of Other Dimensions save Bakr, and recorded a 14-part suite that's unlike any other jazz album, and one of his most fascinating works.

The album is clearly intended to be of a piece, as evidenced by the varying divisions of the ensemble on each track. Not everyone plays at all times. Some pieces are horn duos. Parker has a bass solo. Shipp has a piano solo. Only on one or two occasions does the full quartet play together. The piece takes an almost symmetrical form, beginning with horn duos, moving to solo bass, then a section by the full quartet, followed by a piano solo and another section played by all four musicians. The middle four tracks are, in order, a saxophone-piano duet, horns and bass without Shipp, a saxophone-bass-piano trio, and a trumpet solo. Then the pattern re-emerges, as the lineups of the first five sections are repeated, only in reverse order. The quartet as a whole reforms; Shipp takes another piano solo; the quartet plays again; Parker takes a bass solo; and Campbell and Carter, the horn players, take the ensemble, and the piece, out. Each track is superb on its own, and the suite as a whole is quite remarkable—the absence of a primary rhythm instrument allows the lyrical potential of Shipp's cluster-bomb melodies to expand quite radically. There are many surprises on the disc. Campbell and Carter, playing together, create delicate webs of sound. Parker, on the other hand, uses his first solo to release tight, knotted sonic booms, far from his usual soulful rumble. *Strata* is one of Shipp's favorite albums, and one which shows quite clearly not only the depth of his musical concept, but the room for experimentation contained within it.

Lately, Shipp has talked seriously about retiring from the studio entirely. He continues to record albums, but promises this will peter out by 2001. "I'm trying to [retire]," he says. "I would like to stay out of the studio forever. I have one more album coming out on hat Art...one more String Trio album coming out next year. But I have more stuff out than [alto saxophone and clarinet player] Eric Dolphy had in his entire career. It's like, why keep going? Why? With people slowly coming to me over the years, there's plenty of back catalog for them to absorb. I really feel like I've said what I wanted to say. I'm just really trying to get out of...there's so many albums coming out, I just see the whole thing as like a train with no brakes.

Competing for a small marketplace, the proliferation is too much too fast, and people get egos involved with it, they want every note they've ever played to be documented. For what? Why? There's a part of me that wants to do a solo album and just put it out on my own label and just sell it live with no distribution, and have nothing to do with traditional distribution of jazz, but that would be more of a marketing experiment."

While he doesn't necessarily want to release any more albums of his own music, Shipp is embarking on an enterprise possibly even more interesting in its long-range meaning. He has signed on as the curator of the Blue Series, an imprint of Thirsty Ear, which will release albums by New York's most interesting jazz musicians. So far, the series has included albums by William Parker (in a trio with Daniel Carter and Hamid Drake) and Mat Maneri (a quartet featuring pianist Craig Taborn, Parker and drummer Gerald Cleaver). The inaugural volume, though, was a quartet album under Shipp's leadership, and it is the most surprising album in his discography to date.

Pastoral Composure is the most straight-ahead item in Shipp's catalog. Like the David S. Ware Quartet's *Surrendered,* it's a breathtaking record which, in its embrace of simple (though never simplistic) composition and Modernist concepts of beauty and melody, creates a sound-world even the most tentative listener can fearlessly enter. The transformation is apparent from the first cut. "Gesture," a throbbing Latin-tinged piece, is immediately reminiscent of "Solea," the triumphant finale to the Miles Davis/ Gil Evans album *Sketches Of Spain.* Roy Campbell, playing pocket trumpet and making it sound like a flugelhorn, releases long lines of heartbreaking clarity over the trio's [Shipp, Parker and Cleaver] repetitive, pulsing foundation. The third cut is a version of Duke Ellington's "Prelude To A Kiss," rendered in a significantly more respectful and traditionally beautiful manner than Shipp's wanton demolition of Gershwin's "Summertime" on *Zo,* or the Cubist versions of Ellington's "The 'C' Jam Blues" and "Take The 'A' Train" from *The Multiplication Table*.

Between "Gesture" and "Prelude To A Kiss," though, lies probably the greatest shock in all of Shipp's recorded catalog. "Visions" is a shimmering bop trio cut which dispenses with all avant-garde or 'out' touches and plays like something from a 1958 Blue Note session. It's not a betrayal of his aesthetic; it's an expansion of it, filtered through a complete acknowledgement of tradition and history. And this is emblematic of every aspect of *Pastoral Composure*. By appearing to go backward, Shipp has in fact catapulted himself forward, past all his contemporaries and into the vanguard of current jazz composition. He has proved, unbidden, not only that he can acquit himself, but that he can and will deliver brilliant, lush music in any sub-genre of jazz, and will simultaneously shatter boundaries by force of his artistry alone. "You don't want to be predictable," Shipp says of *Pastoral Composure*. "If you're known for a certain thing the obvious answer in this case is to do something that maybe goes back to your roots, and therefore is organic, too, because it is a part of who you are, even though you don't usually choose to emphasize that when presenting your own personality. But since it's part of your personality, there's no feeling of trying to do something that's not honest. Am I gonna make a career of being a straight-ahead player? No. It's not what I want to do, it's not where I really think the music is, even though I like those compositions and I would perform them onstage in a set. But it just felt right...based on the work [I've] done in the past, to add a specific chapter to the [body of work] that I think is relevant, and it opens a window to [my] vocabulary so I think people can even understand the older albums better. It's [also] a statement of maybe what we feel about how a lot of people are doing straight-ahead music today, not really doing it in a proper spirit and we are, and it's also something else to do in the studio, and that's to me what improvising is, just getting through the day. You're in the studio, how are you gonna get through these hours? I have these tunes, why not record them?"

If *Pastoral Composure* was in some ways a rebellious gesture, showing that Shipp can compete in the straight-ahead jazz arena, his most recent album, *New Orbit,* is something else again. Any attempt to map out a calculated aesthetic strategy will be stymied by this album. Roy Campbell has been replaced on trumpet by Wadada Leo Smith, but the rhythm section of William Parker and Gerald Cleaver returns. Still, though the band is nearly identical to *Pastoral Composure*'s, the albums could not be more different. Where *Pastoral Composure* was smooth and relatively easygoing, *New Orbit* is angular and harsh. Shipp has composed, once again, a series of variations, this time on the "Orbit" theme. The opening cut is the title track, "New Orbit," which is followed throughout the album by "Orbit 2," "3," and "4." Another theme is repeated in "Paradox X" and "Paradox Y." Other cuts bear titles like "Syntax" and "Maze Hint."

It's immediately apparent that trumpeter Smith has taken the music in a thoroughly different direction. His playing is rawer than Campbell's, relying less on streams of high notes and much more on slow, smeared runs. Behind him, Shipp offers jagged, piecemeal melodies, on "Paradox X" plucking the strings to create a harpsichord-like effect which is beautiful, but extraordinarily bleak. Parker also seems to hold himself back throughout the record. Even his bowed solo version of "Orbit 3" is oddly restrained. Normally, Parker's bowed excursions are his most ecstatic, and free, moments on his instrument. But here, his tone is somber, his notes long and mournful. It's an astonishingly beautiful, almost literally breathtaking performance. "Orbit 3" is followed by "U Feature," the only upbeat track on the record, but it doesn't offer more than a momentary respite from the subdued mood which predominates. If, indeed, Shipp intends to retire from the studio, *New Orbit* certainly expresses that desire. Despite its optimistic title, the entire album has the feel of a quiet, dignified farewell.

• William Parker (bass) | Billy Bang (violin)

V • WILLIAM PARKER: BUILDING FROM THE BOTTOM

I t would be almost impossible to imagine the New York free jazz scene without William Parker. The powerful, rock-steady bassist has been playing with anyone and everyone—from Billy Higgins to John Zorn—for nearly thirty years, and has appeared on literally hundreds of albums. He is best known today for his fifteen-year partnership with Matthew Shipp, and his role in the David S. Ware Quartet. But, prior to those endeavors he spent years in Cecil Taylor's various groups. He has also anchored Other Dimensions In Music for nearly two decades, and has recently begun leading his own groups, particularly the Little Huey Creative Music Orchestra and the now-disbanded quartet In Order To Survive. In many ways, William Parker *is* New York free jazz; it's embodied in his tireless music-making, in his serene spirituality, and the welcome he extends to his audiences.

Because he's been around as long as he has, Parker is also a walking history of the music. His memories alone fill huge gaps in what is written about New York's free jazz scene. "Leading into 1975," he told me as we sat in the basement of the club Tonic, "which is ten years after Coltrane did his last quartet recordings, and ten years or so after the Beatles, you had a lot of musicians who were migrating to New York City. In 1973 there was a group we had called the Music Ensemble, which was [violinist] Billy Bang, [saxophonist] Daniel Carter, Dewey Johnson, bassist Earl Freeman, drummer Roger Baird and trumpet player Willie Baraka. And we were playing at Someplace Nice, which was 97 St. Mark's Place, where Yaffa Cafe is today. And we're playing there one Saturday afternoon, and [trombonist] Joe Bowie, Luther Thomas, Luther Petty and [drummer] Charles Bobo Shaw walked in, because they had just gotten in from St. Louis. They sat in with us that afternoon. And shortly after that David Murray arrived [in New York], and quite a number of musicians from St. Louis and Chicago began to arrive in New York. Sam Rivers had a functioning space, very pre-Knitting Factory, called Studio RivBea [where the *Wildflowers* albums were recorded]. That was an artist-owned, artist-operated performance space, and Sam also lived there. That was at 24 Bond Street. You had a place called the Ladies' Fort, run by singer Joely Wilson. You had a place on Second Avenue called Sunrise Studios. There was the National Black Theater, up in Harlem, that we used to work out of. There were lots of places. I guess they call this the 'loft scene,' but there were a lot of places where musicians were putting on concerts...a place called the Firehouse, on 11th Street and Avenue C, was another place. Rashied Ali opened up Ali's Alley shortly after that. Studio We, on Eldridge Street, was open also. There were a lot of independent clubs and independent happenings and places that just popped up. [Composer] Henry Threadgill and [bassist] Fred Hopkins and [drummer] Steve McCall opened up the Air Studio on 13th Street. It was in the air; music, and the idea that you don't wait to be hired, or wait for someone to knock on your door, but create a place. Washington Square Church—the Revolutionary Ensemble, with [violinist] Leroy Jenkins and [bassist] Sirone and [drummer] Jerome Cooper, played there quite frequently. Also [saxophonist] Frank Lowe. Ornette Coleman had a place called Artists House, on Prince Street. Marzette Watts was still around in Cooper Square; he didn't play, but he still lived there, I remember stopping by there. It was very vibrant, as far as people still having the spirit to want to play and think about the short-term business results, meaning that you might play and not make any big money but you wanted to play. The long-term business result would be you wanted to make money and get a wider audience. There were a few people who did independent records. There weren't any record companies, as I recall, in the sense that in the early part of the '70s there was a really big switchover, the radio stations switched over from jazz to soul music, or to country and western. The large record companies, like Columbia and Impulse! and United Artists, they stopped recording jazz and people began to play fusion more, to get into the rock music that was making more money. So you had a whole segment of the music population that was beginning to play rock, to mix jazz and fusion together. So a lot of [free jazz] musicians recorded their own records. They would record them and put them out on their own labels. But slowly, small labels began to materialize, like India Navigation, small European labels, but mostly a lot of it was independent, and a lot of that music didn't make the switch to CD. I mean, [trumpeter] Ted Daniel had a big band at the time called the Energy Ensemble, and they just finally put out a CD of that music. So there was a lot of activity, and people were trying to do their best to play music and survive."

It was from this explosively creative, if largely unheralded, environment that Parker's first album emerged. Like so many others, he released the LP *Through Acceptance Of The Mystery Peace* (the title comes from a Kenneth Patchen poem) on his own label, Centering Records. In 1998, he reissued it on CD through the Massachusetts label Eremite, with one bonus track. The original album contained four lengthy pieces, by ensembles of various sizes— an octet ("Desert Flower"), two different trios ("Commitment" and "Face Still Hands Folded"), and a septet ("Rattles and Bells and the Light of the Sun"). Saxophonist Daniel Carter (later to join Parker in a trio, and in Other Dimensions In Music) appears, as does Toshinori Kondo (with whom Parker would later play in Peter Brötzmann's Die Like A Dog Quartet), violinist Billy Bang, and many others. Very different from the contemporaneous music of the *Wildflowers* sessions, *Through Acceptance...* is a pensive album. Three of the CD's five tracks have no percussion or rhythmic instrumentation; two are arranged primarily for stringed instruments ("Face Still Hands Folded" is a Billy Bang-Ramsey Ameen violin duet with a recitation by Parker, who does not play bass on the track; the title cut features violinists Polly Bradfield and the Far East Side Band's Jason Kao Hwang, cellist Tristan Honsinger and flautist William Connell Jr.—again, Parker does not play on the piece). The opening cut, "Desert Flower," has been expanded to its full length for the CD reissue. It's a throbbing, brass-heavy twenty-minute workout, featuring six reed or brass players (Toshinori Kondo, Will Connell, Jr., Peter Kuhn, Rozanne Levine, Arthur Williams, and Daniel Carter), Denis Charles on drums and Parker on bass. This cut, as early as 1977, gives a vitally important look into Parker's future work with the even larger Little Huey Creative Music Orchestra.

After *Mystery Peace*, Parker did not release another album under his own name until the early 1990s. "I've been doing my own work since the '70s," he says, "[but] it wasn't till the '90s that I said, I'm gonna start a regular band. I've been doing big bands since '72 or '73. It wasn't till 1993 or '94 that I said, well, for business reasons I've got to begin to put out records, I've got to document the work and put it out." It's surprising that, although Parker has appeared in literally hundreds of performing situations with dozens of other musicians over the years, he has less than a dozen albums to his own credit as a leader (all but one released in the last decade). But Parker, for years, has worked more for his own inner artistic satisfaction than for applause or wealth. "Imagine going through your whole life, playing music, doing something you devote your life to, that nobody really gets," he says. "So you say to yourself, well, those that get it, get it. And you also say to yourself, well, what would the world be like if I wasn't doing what I'm doing? Yes, it is important that I'm doing it, and it's not important whether people get it or not, it's important that I do it. And that gets you going to do more. So it's not even our responsibility to worry about it. You have to continue on and find reasons to do what you're doing." This is not to say, of course, that Parker doesn't want everyone in the world to hear his music, and the music of players he admires. "It certainly wouldn't hurt the music if more people heard it," he says. "I know this from playing for senior citizens, and little kids who wouldn't know Charlie Parker if Charlie Parker bit 'em, and they wouldn't know Miles Davis and they wouldn't know Thelonious Monk, but they hear this music and they like it. Having known nothing about it. So I know that people can dig this music. And if we've got...ten percent [of the jazz] audience that listen to it, there's probably 30, 40 percent more people who would love it if they knew it existed. They're waiting for this music, but it's hard to get it to them. The salvation is not in the people who listen to the music, the salvation is in the people who don't listen to the music."

If Parker seeks to convert people to his music, his biggest project, the Little Huey Creative Music Orchestra, is the equivalent of total-immersion baptism. The Orchestra, which varies in size from twelve to twenty-plus members, plays to a packed house at each year's Vision Festival, and kicked off the 2000 Festival with a parade through the East Village which drew people from their homes to march through the streets to the New Age Cabaret, where performances were held for the next eleven nights. Later in the week, Little Huey performed a nearly hour-long piece, "Kaleidoscope," in which blaring brass charts alternated with the gentle sifting sound of all the members lifting and shaking African rainsticks (hollow poles filled with seeds, which create a whooshing, rattling sound as the sticks are tipped from one end to the other). The audience was rapt for the entire performance. All conversation ceased, and when Parker and his orchestra were finished conjuring their music, the ceiling echoed with the vast eruption of love and admiration which followed.

Over the course of three releases (*Flowers Grow In My Room*, on Centering, and the Aum Fidelity releases *Sunrise In The Tone World* and *Mayor Of Punkville*) the Orchestra has created some of the most overwhelming music to be found anywhere. Both of the Aum Fidelity releases are double discs, and both are live albums. *Sunrise In The Tone World* was recorded at numerous shows over more than a year, while *Mayor Of Punkville* was recorded over the course of several months in 1999, when the Orchestra performed every Sunday at Tonic. Little Huey's recorded repertoire ranges from throbbing, Mingus-esque marches to delicate tone poems; from blaring brass assaults to slow, lush balladry behind a gentle vocalist. This range is particularly well documented on *Punkville*. On "James Baldwin To The Rescue," for example, singer Aleta Hayes delivers a melancholy, gospel-tinged lyric written by Parker, which somehow remains filled with life and joy. "I know it must be hard to be named after God," she sings. "I wish I may I wish I might be anything I want tonight…Your life is ending only to begin." Similarly, "Interlude #7 (Huey's Blues)," which opens Disc Two, is one of the most beautiful pieces of music released by anyone in the 1990s—a slow vamp which brings to mind images and thoughts of darkness, not as a threat but as a warm place in which to enfold yourself and feel safe; the piece embodies that magical aspect of the blues which allows it to be both mournful and celebratory at once. Easily the most astonishing, and overpowering, cut on the entire album is "I Can't Believe I Am Here." A nearly half-hour workout, it contains so much sheer brass power (a total of thirteen players: three trumpets, three trombones, a tuba, and six saxophones ranging from soprano to baritone), that by the time the piece concludes with a skull-crushing, spine-rattling, drum solo from Andrew Barker, the listener is utterly exhausted and totally at the kind of peace that only comes from a hard day of physical labor.

And though *Mayor Of Punkville* is a particularly powerful and beautiful statement, according to Parker the Orchestra's output to date represents only the smallest fraction of its repertoire, and its capabilities. "I'm not really sure whether I had an idea where it was going [when I began it]," he says, "but I know that it's still, which is the great thing about it, it's still the tip of the iceberg in terms of where it's gonna go. Because we've just really begun. We don't get enough opportunities to play. I've got boxes and boxes of music at home, and if we ever could get it together to play for a long time, we've got quite a repertoire and a range. If you heard Little Huey on

Monday, you could say 'I heard that Little Huey Orchestra,' and if somebody saw them on Tuesday, they'd say 'Are we talking about the same band?' It's the same band, yes, but at the same time we're really reaching a wide scope of music. It's moving along, is all I really can say, I mean, I don't know where I really want it to go except where it wants to go. I don't really have a sound. All we're trying to do is bring everybody [in the Orchestra] up to a level of their playing and working together, to the highest place it can go. What the music will sound like, I don't know, but that's what we're shooting for."

The same level of instrumental achievement, albeit in more intimate, focused forms, is apparent on Parker's albums featuring In Order To Survive and his recent trio album, *Painter's Spring* (Thirsty Ear). In Order To Survive, a quartet which Parker disbanded in early 2000, featured Rob Brown on alto saxophone, Cooper-Moore (once of David S. Ware's group Apogee) on piano, and former Ware Quartet drummer Susie Ibarra. They released three albums: *Compassion Seizes Bed-Stuy* (Homestead), *The Peach Orchard* (Aum Fidelity), and *Posium Pendasem* (FMP). Just to be confusing, there is an earlier Parker album called *In Order To Survive* (FMP), which predates the quartet but features Rob Brown and Cooper-Moore, alongside trombonist Grachan Moncur II, trumpet player Lewis Barnes, percussionist Jackson Krall, and drummer Denis Charles. "It was a very popular band," Parker says of the quartet. This may be due to the relative simplicity of the group's music. His compositions for In Order To Survive albums were often blues-based, or rooted in relatively easy-to-grasp melodic structures from which solos emerged gradually and naturally, without the impression of swirling, roaring chaos that Little Huey sometimes assaults the unprepared ear with. "It didn't feel like an eternal thing, like it'd last forever, but it could return," he says. "I was just thinking the other day about putting the quartet back together. I think basically, for this particular period, things had kind of run their course. It just felt right to take a break from things for awhile, and let people do their own thing, and then at some point come back, maybe. I don't know. I don't usually repeat things and go back, but maybe going back may mean going forward." For the moment, though, his focus, at least as a leader, is on larger ensemble structures. The trio with whom he recorded *Painter's Spring* (Thirsty Ear), for example, is not a working band, although this may be due to simple logistics—drummer Hamid Drake, a crucial element in the group's sound, lives in Chicago.

Parker's work with Drake has become increasingly recognized of late. The two spur each other to dizzying performance heights, both live and in the studio. This is particularly noticeable on *Painter's Spring* and *Two Days In April* (an album the pair recorded with saxophonists Fred Anderson and "Kidd" Jordan, on Eremite), but performances by Peter Brötzmann's Die Like A Dog Quartet, and quartet albums like *From Valley To Valley* (Eremite) and the twin volumes of *Little Birds Have Fast Hearts* (FMP), provide even more evidence that Parker and Drake are one of the most potent, and shockingly groove-oriented, rhythm sections in free jazz. Not since Ronald Shannon Jackson has a drummer gone so deep in the pocket as Drake. About this, Parker is typically dry, penetrating straight through any rhetoric with his own observations of the partnership. "A lot of people are writing, it's surprising that William is doing this or doing that," he says. "But in 1973, I was playing every day with [drummer] Billy Higgins. I'd go to his house and we'd play duets every day. And the way I play with Hamid is basically the way that I've always played. Not that these people have heard me play this way, they've heard me play contrapuntal rhythms and polyrhythmic things, but basically Hamid, I can get a groove with that's both in the pocket, out of the pocket, free and beyond all at the same time. So basically, we have a good groove system going, and it can just flow from one rhythm to another to another to another. Which is the same concept I used with Cecil Taylor, by the way, except that we [Parker and Drake] use what you would call long repetitions, whereas with Cecil we might play a groove for three seconds one minute, then it goes to another one, then it goes to another one. With Hamid, we play the rhythm changes in...longer cycles, so you hear it, and your musical memory and your rhythm memory recognize it and feel the pulse. It's trance music. It's repetition. See, when things are changing all the time, it works a different set of senses, and that's why people say, well, I don't hear any rhythm. Because it's not separated out. But it's also the way he plays, the feel that he has, which is really, really fantastic."

This is amply demonstrated on *Painter's Spring,* which (along with Matthew Shipp's *Pastoral Composure,* the David S. Ware Quartet's *Surrendered,* and *Two Days In April*) is part of a recent wave of incredibly swinging recent free jazz albums. The record opens like the producer fired a starter's pistol; "Foundation #1" is a maze of thrumming bass, whip-cracking drum patterns, and Daniel Carter's saxophone slicing away acerbically at the melody. Every composition on the record is strongly blues- or gospel-rooted, and all except one demonstrate the amazing groove-making powers of Parker and Drake. The sole exception is a solo bass version of the spiritual "There Is A Balm In Gilead," which Parker plays with a bow. He conjures deep, resonant tones in the piece, and only rarely heads into the bass' upper range. The result is practically despairing, like the work of classical composers Arvo Pärt and Henryk Goreçki, yet Parker's own spiritual joy still comes through. It's an incredible record, one all the more astounding because of the micro-focus the trio allows the listener. Where Parker can sometimes be lost in a Little Huey tidal-wave of sound, or even remove himself entirely and merely conduct, on *Painter's Spring* he is one-third of an all-star triangle of talent, and it's one of his best records. The only records comparable to it, for sheer concentration of power, are two records he made with Charles Gayle—*Touchin' On Trane* (FMP), which features Rashied Ali on drums, and *Kingdom Come* (Knitting Factory), which features Sunny Murray behind the kit. For all the admitted power of these drummers, though (and *Touchin' On Trane,* in particular, has a hell of a reputation even in mainstream books like the *Penguin Guide To Jazz On CD*), the Parker-Drake rhythm section is one of the best in jazz, and bears marvelous sonic fruit every time its two members unite.

The relationship between the two is explored as microscopically as it could ever be on the Aum Fidelity CD *Piercing The Veil*, which is simply a series of duets between the two players. Forty-five minutes of bass-drum duets could intimidate any listener, so it's fortunate the disc is much more varied than that. The opening cut is a throbbing, convulsive rhythm line that any reed or brass player would rejoice over having behind them, but with no trumpet or saxophone there, the interaction between Drake and Parker is simply mind-blowing. It's pure dance music—indeed, it's easy to close your eyes and picture the smiles on the players' faces as they crank the sound up and out, never losing the groove but taking it to a place where ecstasy takes over from intellect. Other cuts on the disc head into substantially different territory. Parker plays some selections with a bow, and on others abandons the bass entirely—two pieces feature him blowing a Middle Eastern or North African reed instrument while Drake plays the tablas. The effect is trance-inducing and meditative. This album proves that the most minimal instrumentation can sometimes provide the most awe-inspiring results, particularly in the hands of master musicians like Parker and Drake.

Parker has also recently released a more traditional record, *O'Neal's Porch,* on his own Centering Records label. A quartet session, the disc features Drake again on drums, and a front line of Rob Brown on alto saxophone and Lewis Barnes on trumpet. Brown is particularly impressive here, playing with more fire and energy than at almost any point in his career. He's quite often a refined, laid-back player; on this disc, though, he cuts loose from the first notes of the opening cut, "Purple." His saxophone and Barnes' trumpet come together in wild arpeggios and unison riffs, as the rhythm section churns beneath them. The whole album (eight cuts in 72 minutes) is a triumphantly swinging chunk of sound. The compositions, all Parker originals, expand on the bluesy strut of In Order To Survive's best work, creating a musical atmosphere that practically demands a kinetic response. "Rise," a throbbing blues-based vamp, sounds like it could have come from the pen of Charles Mingus. Building from a terrific hard-bop melody into a crashing, heart-stopping drum solo from Hamid Drake, the piece is one of the highlights of the disc. Every track here is a keeper. Particularly fascinating are the two versions of the simple melody "Song For Jesus," which appears here as a tender, subtle ballad and then, two tracks later, as a romping blowout ("Song For Jesus 3/4"). Parker clearly wants people to enjoy this music on many levels—to think about it, yes, but to feel it in their hearts, and dance to it, too. John Philip Sousa said, "Jazz will endure as long as people hear it with their feet instead of their brains," and this music will surely endure in the hearts, and the feet, of anyone who hears it.

His capacity for swing is only one facet of Parker's playing. He can hold his own in almost any musical situation, often surpassing those around him even when playing by their rules rather than his own. Through his work with Cecil Taylor, among others, he's been exposed to a wide variety of European players, and formed long-time, productive musical relationships on both sides of the Atlantic. Peter Brötzmann's Die Like A Dog Quartet is an anomaly, being composed of three Americans (Roy Campbell, Parker, and Drake) alongside the red-faced, leather-lunged German reed-master. Die Like A Dog's music, consequently, is very groove-oriented and blues-based, providing the "trance" effect discussed above. But the vast majority of European players come from a far more aesthetically dispassionate school of improvisation, arising more from a modern classical tradition than from jazz (which is, after all, a music created for the most part by black Americans). Parker's gentle demeanor, and openness of spirit, allows him to embrace the Europeans as musical equals, and fellows (one of his more interesting sessions was John Zorn's album *Harras,* which featured Zorn, Parker, and British guitarist Derek Bailey), though he seems to disagree with their attempts to excise spirituality from the music. He views spirituality as central.

"Music is bigger than us all," he says. "Even though one may say we [American free jazz artists] acknowledge a certain spirit of the music, or a spirituality in the music, where other musicians don't wish to deal with any aesthetic thing put on the music like 'spirit of the music,' they want to keep it just music, dry, or very sharply cut. But you can't keep the superhuman spirit of life out of music. So whether one says I'm playing trance music, or cosmic music, or I'm playing music because I'm trying to raise the level of consciousness of people, I'm trying to open people's third ear and eye...it happens in all musics. When musicians in Tibet play, it happens when musicians in the street or in the park play. I think a lot of European musicians don't get into the spirituality of the music. They don't talk about that. They don't really acknowledge that part of it. They just want to play free improvisation. But when you play free improvisation, I think God is there too. The spirit is there too. Whether you like it or not. It's not up to you, the musician, to say 'I don't believe in this,' or 'I don't want to deal with that,' because we aren't the masters of the music. The music is bigger than us, and it's there whether we want it to be or not."

Spiritual differences aside, Parker is open to new situations because of the ever-present possibility of transcendence through sound, which is the purpose to which he has set himself on Earth. "It works as a peripheral thing sometimes when you play with different musicians from around the world. Sometimes it really sings, when you have people working on the same level. You can hear the difference, you can feel the difference. When you hear a good R&B band that's working, versus one that's not working. The one that doesn't work, it will work sometimes, but...a master musician, every time he picks up the instrument it works on some level. It's not serendipitous. It works because that's what you've devoted your life to." Still, though, he is critical of musicians who don't have the same reverence he does. He feels that this stifles them creatively. "If you devote your life to getting Cs," he says, "then every time you play, you'll get Cs," referring to an academic grade, not a note. "And if you devote your life to getting an A++ every time you play, that'll be your grounding point. When you're playing, and you're European or whatever you are, and you come to a melody, and you say 'No, I can't play a melody,' or 'We can't swing, we can't play a groove, because then it's no longer free improvisation, it's jazz, and we don't want to play jazz,' it's the same as a so-called jazz musician that's playing bebop and all of a sudden the bebop is gone and you're playing free jazz. The Charlie Parker tune is gone, you left that behind ten minutes ago. And you start saying 'We can't go there because then we won't be playing jazz.' That's the same crime as someone who's playing free music and runs into the blues licks and won't play them because of their fear of sounding like some jazz guy. So I think it's a choice that you make, and everyone has got their low points and their high points in what they do, but people choose which camp they want to be in and they choose how far they want to go. And you are what you train yourself to be or to do. Charles Gayle is one thing, but then a guy like [straight-ahead saxophonist] Joe Lovano, that's another thing. But people pick what they do. Everyone chooses what they want to listen to and what they want to do and who they want to follow. Those that cross over and play with everybody, you learn to make the best of different situations. You find the swinging point, or the point where people are trying to make music together. Sometimes it works, and then sometimes you never want to play with those people again, because you feel that it doesn't work. There is a difference of aesthetics, there are differences of cultures, as far as how they live, who they are, where they're from, what they believe in, all [this] affects the music and it affects whether other people want to play with them."

• Roy Campbell

VI • ROY CAMPBELL: ATOP THE PYRAMID

The common myth is that trumpet players are egotistical and arrogant by nature. This is in no small part due to the legacy of Miles Davis, a clear runner-up for the title of Meanest Man In Music, if not the all-time winner. Certainly, it takes a particular temperament to convince yourself you can lead a band with only the small voice of the trumpet. In its uppermost register, the horn makes a shrill, pinched tone, nothing like the low-end bellow of a tenor saxophone, or the shimmering waves of sound a pianist can conjure. It's a difficult instrument to master. Few are willing to commit themselves to it. Trumpeters are a rare commodity, in New York and everywhere else, and particularly in free jazz. When I told tenor saxophonist Assif Tsahar that I had once played the trumpet, but had given it up to pursue writing, his face fell. Only half-jokingly, he told me in an urgent voice "You should start again! Everybody's looking for trumpet players nowadays!"

Roy Campbell has gained his prominent place in the New York jazz scene by filling every empty trumpet chair he can. Campbell, a stocky, perpetually smiling man, is practically omnipresent. "A lot of people come to me and say 'Man, we see your name everywhere. How'd you do that!?'," Campbell told me with a laugh. "One day, [tenor saxophonist] Frank Lowe asked me 'Who's your press agent?' and I told him God." His temperament, though, hardly matches the arrogance of the mythic jazz trumpeter. Instead, like Clifford Brown or Dizzy Gillespie, Campbell is a gentle and friendly man. He can be found holding court each year at the Vision Festival, in animated conversation with anyone who wants to stop and talk.

And when he hits the bandstand, his love of music and life is clear with every note of his horn.

Campbell has three major bands. He performs each Monday night with his group Tazz, at the Lenox Lounge in Harlem. For a half-dozen years, he's been playing standards and blowing the blues for a mixed crowd of locals and tourists, from around the country and around the world. From time to time, he plays dates with bassist William Parker in the Pyramid Trio. There have been many drummers in the Pyramid Trio—Zen Matsuura was the first, followed by Reggie Nicholson, Susie Ibarra, and Michael Zerang. The trio's third and latest CD, *Ethnic Stew And Brew* (Delmark), features Hamid Drake behind the kit. And finally, he is one of the four members of Other Dimensions In Music. Other Dimensions is an improvisational quartet, so there's no actual leader, but Campbell shares the front line with saxophonist Daniel Carter (who plays a little trumpet himself from time to time). This list doesn't include his sometime projects, like the nine-piece Tazz Concert Ensemble or his Coltrane tribute project, Shades And Colors Of Trane. Other Dimensions In Music has been together since 1981, and the Pyramid Trio since 1983. When Campbell starts a group, it's always with the understanding that the music he's creating there may well require investigation and exploration for the rest of his life.

Campbell also works as a sideman, in dozens of contexts. He is one of the trumpeters in William Parker's mammoth Little Huey Creative Music Orchestra. He appears on Matthew Shipp's recent *Pastoral Composure,* and played on the pianist's 1997 CD *Strata.* Campbell has replaced Toshinori Kondo in Peter Brötzmann's Die Like A Dog Quartet, and can be heard on that group's live CD, *From Valley To Valley* (Eremite). He's also a member of alto saxophonist Rob Brown's quartet, playing on the recent CD *Jumping Off The Page* (No More). But Campbell's career stretches beyond free jazz, and even beyond New York, and the United States, to Europe and beyond. "I also play with Latin bands, reggae bands,

R&B bands, rock bands, you name it," Campbell says. "I've played with Middle Eastern musicians, European musicians, African musicians."

Much of this willingness to shatter any boundary, whether geographical or musical, which might limit his playing comes from Campbell's childhood, and his studies. "When I studied music, I studied a lot of records," he explains. "When I was in college, in Yusef [Lateef]'s course Music And World Cultures, I used to go to the Lincoln Center library [to listen to records]...I always liked Eastern music and Spanish bolero music, from the time I was a child. I used to watch TV and check out movies, and I wouldn't just be into the flick. I would be into the soundtracks, too. I remember when I was a kid, seeing *Ali Baba And The Forty Thieves,* and *Sabu,* and *Zorro,* and all that kind of stuff. I was very into that, and it's influenced my music, too. Some of the music I compose, people say it sounds like soundtracks."

Campbell, born in 1952, began playing music at a very early age, but didn't pick up the trumpet till he was 17. "I had had piano lessons when I was about six to about eight years old," he says, "and then in elementary school I played flute and recorder, and in junior high school I played violin for about three years or so. I wasn't really into the violin. I wanted to play saxophone, or some type of horn, back then. If I did play a stringed instrument, I wanted to play string bass, but the teacher wouldn't allow me a choice of instrument. He thought I would be a good violin player, because I had a perfect score in music on tests, and also I had perfect pitch. So that's why they wanted me to play violin."

When he finally picked up the instrument that would shape his life, though, Campbell got off to a rocketing start, and came under the influence of a wide range of excellent teachers. "I started playing trumpet in 1970," he remembers, "and by 1971 I was in top 40 [cover] bands, playing Kool & The Gang, and James Brown, and by 1973 I had a jazz band of my own. I was also going to school at that time, attending Manhattan Community College, majoring in music. I was also going to the Jazzmobile Workshop, and the Jazz Interactions Workshop. [Trumpeters] Joe Newman, Lee Morgan, Kenny Dorham, and Howard McGhee used to teach there. I studied in group sessions with Lee Morgan. I used to go to a lot of his shows in the late '60s, and up until the time he died [in 1972]. We talked about music, and how you should know how to play changes, and play the blues. He used to give different exercises on the blackboards. I also studied classical music with Joe Newman. When I was in college I majored in trumpet. I studied with Dick Vance, who was [pianist and bandleader] Fletcher Henderson's trumpet player when he was 18 years old. I also studied composition with [saxophonist] Yusef Lateef."

All these teachers contributed various concepts and elements to Campbell's style and compositional focus, as he developed. Yusef Lateef's integration of Asian and Middle Eastern melodic and tonal structures into jazz undoubtedly influenced Campbell's efforts in similar directions, just as Howard McGhee's stylistic blending of Armstrong-style traditional jazz with the modern bop idiom must have informed the young player's integration of all of trumpet history into his playing. But it is certainly Lee Morgan who seems to have had the greatest influence on the teenaged Roy Campbell, both in terms of melodic orientation and sheer instrumental technique.

Morgan rose quickly to fame in the mid-1950s, winning comparisons to Clifford Brown when he was only 18. Though he, like Brown, didn't live as long as he should have—he was shot to death at Slug's Saloon in 1972—Morgan released a flood of albums on the Blue Note and Savoy labels during his lifetime. He also appeared on literally dozens of sessions with other players, most notably saxophonist Hank Mobley, and as part of Art Blakey's Jazz Messengers. Most of the Blakey, Mobley and Morgan albums are now reissued on CD. These reissues—including albums under Morgan's leadership like *The Sidewinder, Cornbread* and *Search For*

The New Land—contain some of the most brilliant hard bop playing of the 1950s and 1960s.

One of the most notable things about Morgan's trumpet style was his tremendous sense of melody. This shows up very strongly in Campbell's playing as well. Campbell goes much further out with his sonic concepts than Morgan ever did, but the melody is always there as an anchor, tying him back to the hard bop of the 1950s, and even earlier periods. Campbell expresses great admiration for players of the 1930s, who he feels don't get the notice they deserve from listeners of today. "Coleman Hawkins and Henry 'Red' Allen...they'd be playing tunes, and in between they'd play some runs and some phrases that were crazy, completely out of the tune. Like, some free stuff. And then they'd go right back into the tune. And a lot of people are not aware of that music they were doing back then," he says, and goes on to list other important players of the pre-war era. "I like Fats Navarro [a major influence on Clifford Brown and Lee Morgan], Benny Bailey, and Idris Sulieman, and they were all trumpet players who came up in the 1940s." Campbell, like many of the new-to-jazz fans of his music, is constantly looking for something he's never heard before. Like Matthew Shipp and William Parker and David Ware, he understands the urge the new crop of free jazz listeners are feeling to explore jazz in all its facets.

"I used to listen to traditional music," he explains, "and when I got to be about 15, I started listening to avant-garde music too. I'd listen to Trane, and I met [drummer] Sunny Murray in 1967. He played with Byard Lancaster at Carnegie Hall, and Sunny did a solo that...I was just astounded by all the sound and rhythm he was getting just out of a snare drum and a ride cymbal. That's all he was playing at the time. And then, when I started listening to Albert Ayler's music, I saw that jazz was like a circle. You start from New Orleans music, go to big band music, to bebop and swing, and then you had cool jazz...but when I heard Albert Ayler's music, it was like a complete circle. The beginning and the end at the same time. Because you would hear some of his music that was like folk themes,

New Orleans march themes, and then they would go off into some other harmonics and other sounds. I really liked Donald Ayler [Albert's brother, who played trumpet]. I also listened to Don Cherry, Philip Dixon, I was into the Art Ensemble of Chicago. I saw them the first time they came to New York. They came to Central Park, and then they played a spot in Brooklyn called the East, that was like a black cultural center in the late 1960s or early 1970s."

New listeners can always find an easy entrance to free jazz through Roy Campbell's music because, like them, he is an explorer, always looking for the next sound while retaining all that links it to what's come before. This musical curiosity manifests itself in two major ways—first, the variety of contexts in which he plays, and second, in his exploitation of the whole family of trumpet-based instruments. "I play pocket trumpet too," he says, "and I've got some other kinda stuff on that. My embouchure [the way a player's lips shape themselves to the horn's mouthpiece] is...open and loose. I get stuff on that pocket trumpet that I can't even hear on the flugelhorn. See, all those instruments, even though they're in the same family, they have distinct voices, and distinct tones, and there's different things you can do with them. Cause I play cornet also, but most of the time I don't play that in public. But every now and then when I make a recording, I always record at least one or two tunes on cornet. A pocket trumpet is like a soprano saxophone, and a flugelhorn is like a tenor saxophone, and a trumpet is, like, related to an alto." The saxophone comparisons lead Campbell to a confession, though: "I really wanted to be a tenor saxophone player," he says, "but I'm glad I didn't become a saxophone player, because if I had, I would have been chasing Trane all my life. Cause I loved Trane so much, I would have probably wanted to sound like that, and I would have been studying his runs, practicing his solos, and I might not have developed my own voice." Campbell needn't worry about that anymore. He's a unique voice in jazz, and his playing is almost immediately recognizable, whether he's appearing as a sideman on an almost hard-bop disc like Matthew Shipp's *Pastoral*

Composure, or releasing the wild free-blowing sound-streams of Other Dimensions In Music. But, his voice is most clearly articulated on his albums as a leader.

Communion (Silkheart, 1994), the first album by the Pyramid Trio, is a perfect example of Campbell's fusion of the avant-garde with the hard bop of his youth. The title track, a William Parker composition which opens the disc, centers around a very Ornette Coleman-esque melody line and a hard-swinging rhythm pattern from Parker and drummer Reggie Nicholson. Campbell's initial solo repeats the melody just enough times to embed it in the listener's memory; then it's gone, and he's off into the upper registers of his horn. Throughout the piece, Campbell plays near the top of the trumpet's range, yet he never seems to lose control or vanish into painful, dog-whistle squealing. (This is a very difficult balance to maintain—on the *Complete Live At The Plugged Nickel* boxed set, for example, even Miles Davis quite often turns high notes into awkward squeaks.) When Campbell steps away from the microphone and Parker solos, he maintains the extraordinarily high energy level the trumpeter has set. The bassist never reaches for his bow, never risks losing the momentum of the piece. Instead, Parker plucks steadily, incrementally up the bass's range, Reggie Nicholson adding drum accents behind him until the tension becomes almost unbearable. Only then does Campbell return, with another skyrocketing blast of high notes to lead into the closing melodic restatement. The rest of *Communion's* tracks are also furious, hard-bop blowouts. Even "Chant For Don Cherry," a tribute to the former Ornette Coleman collaborator and one-world musical pioneer, stays well within the parameters of what even the newest listener would, without a second thought, recognize as jazz.

The second volume of Pyramid Trio work is something different. *Ancestral Homeland* (No More, 1998) is much more a world-music album. The track titles provide an instant clue as to Campbell's intentions for the session—these include "Ancestral Homeland," "Oglala Eclipse," "Camel Caravan" and, most tellingly, "Brother

Yusef," a two-part tribute to Yusef Lateef. Lateef was, of course, another early pioneer in the combination of ethnic (particularly African) sounds into jazz, and the first part of this suite is an utterly alien-sounding four minutes—drummer Zen Matsuura and Parker both play percussion, and Campbell plays sinuous, desert-inflected lines on the argol, a Middle Eastern or North African reed instrument. The second half of "Brother Yusef" is played with traditional jazz instrumentation, but the melody retains its North African flavor. Matsuura, actually the Pyramid Trio's original drummer, is much more willing to head into the realms of exotic percussion than Nicholson was on the previous disc; the title track, for example, features much more hand percussion than traditional drumming, and Campbell expands his own sonic palette on the track, playing wood flute and percussion. Parker, too, plays percussion instead of bass on a few tracks. *Ancestral Homeland* is the most introspective of the three Pyramid Trio discs. There are many moments of near-inaudibility during its 75-minute running time, as the musicians explore realms much more spiritual than bombastic.

Not so *Ethnic Stew And Brew* (Delmark, 2001). Though the trio's latest drummer, Hamid Drake, has his own uses for ethnic percussion instruments, particularly tablas and bongos, and is right at home playing non-jazz rhythms, this album is a terrifically energetic, groove-oriented workout. The Delmark recording date was booked after a label representative saw the three backing Peter Brötzmann as part of the Die Like A Dog Quartet, and that level of full-blooded interaction is what's represented here. The first cut, "Tazz's Dilemma," is built around a throbbing, hypnotic William Parker bassline, to which Drake adds perfect accents, coming down hard on the snare and sending the whole trio skittering forward like whipped horses. Campbell skyrockets to the topmost range of the horn, releasing shimmering runs which devolve into smeared abstraction in the middle but return to pristine clarity before diving back to earth. Of the disc's seven tracks, only "Impressions Of Yokohama" contains any nontraditional sonic touches. (On the cut,

William Parker plays the Japanese shakuhachi flute, quite beautifully.) Clearly, given the stripped-down trio format, this group is the closest project to Campbell's heart, and expresses what he wants to say about jazz, and about music as a whole, in the most explicit terms. The main message coming through from even the first listen to *Ethnic Stew And Brew,* though, is that the Pyramid Trio is one of the most convulsively swinging small jazz groups in the country. Blues-based but world-savvy, their music, as with all the best jazz, aims to change the way you walk, and succeeds admirably.

Campbell's command of the trumpet's uppermost range is one of the most immediately noticeable elements of his style. Few players in current jazz, whether mainstream or avant-garde, have his level of control on the high notes. Fewer still can make the transitions he makes, going into the stratosphere, almost past the level of human hearing, and then returning smoothly to the middle range without fluffing a note. In the Dizzy Gillespie bebop era, when high notes were often the yardstick for measuring instrumental virtuosity, Campbell would have been worshipped. "I studied with another teacher, David Snor," Campbell says about this almost preternatural talent of his, "and he showed me a method to build up high notes. I had already worked on that in a certain sense, and he just extended it further when I started studying with him. It's a mouth pressure technique. And I think also, from playing the violin, playing the trumpet and the flute, I tend to hear a lot of the high notes. But I don't play high notes for the sake of technique. A certain type of intensity comes with high notes. Also, it's not an easy job to do that. What I do, most people consider it very phenomenal. Miles Davis asked Dizzy Gillespie years ago, 'how do you get all those high notes?' And Dizzy said you have to hear them in order to execute them."

Campbell sees his upper-register work, like so much else about his playing, as part of the overall musical continuum of jazz, and even the music that makes up the world itself. "I'm always listening to birds' tunes. And birds sing in registers that are extremely high," he says. Continuing to talk about his influences, he adds, "There was a trumpet player who played with Lionel Hampton's band named Leo 'Whistler' Shepherd, I think it was in the late 1940s. And I had bought this record, and all of a sudden at the end of some of these tunes this guy would play a solo, and he was higher than [Duke Ellington trumpeter] Cat Anderson! I also knew Hannibal Marvin Peterson, and he could play a lot of high notes with a lot of energy. Freddie Hubbard, also. All these guys influenced me. I used to play with Woody Shaw and Hannibal, we used to practice together and hang out together, hear music together." Another factor which separates Campbell from most other trumpet players is his pursuit of "outside" sounds on the horn. "To play this genre of music," he says, "you have to have some kind of imagination. It's not all about technique. Eventually you have to get into sound. A lot of people study these instruments [in the trumpet family], and they're not into sound. The guys from straightahead, like Wynton Marsalis, and Roy Hargrove, and Wallace Roney—they're good players, technically, but they just play the instrument. They're not exploring other types of sounds. I've developed the trumpet into something like a synthesizer. I play music, and I also get a lot of different sounds out of it too. I was into Jimi Hendrix, and I always felt that they invented the synthesizer behind what Hendrix was able to do with all those Marshall amps, getting all the different sounds. Because you notice that a couple of years after Jimi passed away, all of a sudden synthesizers had developed."

Campbell's interest in the rawer edges of the trumpet gets a thorough going-over on the Rob Brown Quartet CD *Jumping Off The Page* (No More). The album consists of eight compositions by alto saxophonist Brown, and plays like the most explicit tribute to the 1959-61 Ornette Coleman quartet I've ever heard. The melodic statements played in unison that begin many pieces (particularly the album opener, "Twinkle") are practically pure Coleman in the way they slide up and down scales before the rhythm section (Chris Lightcap on bass and Jackson Krall on drums) leaps in, swinging.

Campbell's playing seems to deliberately echo Don Cherry's short, sharp squiggles of notes. He smears his lines, sometimes biting riffs off before they can resolve themselves and other times allowing them to dissolve into burps and grinding sounds. It's a fascinatingly ugly vision of the trumpet, taking the "growling" effects of the 1920s to a new and nightmarish extreme. At the same time, though, the album retains enough melodic prettiness to make it consistently pleasurable, and never just a listener endurance test. It's a weird, if possibly too-easy-to-overlook, tangent in Campbell's discography.

Within Other Dimensions In Music, Campbell's trumpet gets its most unfettered workouts. The quartet plays such a range of music that every aspect of his voice can be heard, at one point or another, even during a single performance. He formed the group in 1981, primarily in order to work with his longtime friend, saxophonist Daniel Carter. "I met Daniel Carter in 1974," Campbell says. "I had a band that used to rehearse on 19th Street, with a female singer and a piano player. We used to call that band the Spirits Of Rhythm. She knew Daniel from Stonybrook, or some college, and she invited Daniel to the rehearsals. And he came to several of our rehearsals, and he wasn't playing the tunes, but I could hear that he could play. I could hear what he was doing. And that's where our relationship started. He did a large orchestra thing that played on WKCR [Columbia University's radio station]. There's one tape of it, there's another tape that's missing. He just had a bunch of musicians from all kinds of backgrounds. This was like October of 1974. I participated in that, and then me and him didn't play together for a while, but we used to talk on the phone. And then, when I started playing with [saxophonist] Jemeel Moondoc, we somehow got reacquainted, musically, again. Jemeel had this group called the Big Moon Ensemble, it was a double quartet...Arthur Williams played, and myself, Daniel, Jay Oliver was on bass, Dennis Charles was on drums, Rashid Bakr was on drums...we played at St. Marks Church. That was a very good concert. Then Jemeel went to stay in Germany for a while in 1981 and 1982, and I used to lead a jam session in this place called Studio 97. An after-hours jam session; we used to start about two AM and go till nine or ten the next day on the weekends. But after Jemeel left, I said to William [Parker] and Rashid, we still gotta play, so let's form a group with Daniel, and that's how Other Dimensions In Music came into existence."

Though Other Dimensions In Music have played together off and on since 1981, with no changes in membership, they didn't make their recorded debut until 1988, on Silkheart. The self-titled album holds nothing back. On vinyl, it contained two side-long tracks; the CD adds two more pieces from the same session, for a total of just over 70 minutes of music. I heard it after I was already familiar with the group's other two CDs, but it may be my favorite. Unlike their second disc, the debut has no fadeouts—pieces run their full course. Each musician states his case fully and beautifully. Campbell's, Carter's and especially William Parker's playing is forceful, aggressive and at the same time introspective and melancholy.

Even on this early disc, there is a sense of almost telepathic communication that is nearly unique in contemporary music, particularly in a fully improvisational context. It's sometimes hard to believe, listening to cuts like the 23-minute "Tradition's Transitional Omissions Suite—Sailing Towards The Dark Happy Voice" or the 16-minute "Sihu Chant For Sly Stone", that these musical concepts sprang from nothing more than the inspiration of the moment. The CD is even more revelatory when the listener considers the way even some of the greatest jazz groups seem to stiffen up in the recording studio, finding themselves incapable of the kind of unfettered brilliance that seems to come naturally in front of an audience. Truly, this debut recording proved, from the moment it emerged, that Other Dimensions In Music were one of the best groups in New York, if not in all of jazz. Sadly, the disc has slipped almost entirely through the cracks. At the time of its release, nobody had heard of the group outside of New York, and the record was sparsely reviewed, at best. These days, it's a lucky jazz fan who can find the thing in stores, though it's still in print. Anyone who spots it would do well to snap it up without a second thought.

It wasn't until nearly nine years later that the group's potential would be fully revealed to a larger public. In 1997, Aum Fidelity released *Now!*, the second Other Dimensions recording. In some ways it was a logical progression, but it was also significantly different from the first album. Still, from the opening notes of the half-hour-plus "For The Glass Tear (After Evening's Orange)," the power of the quartet was inescapable. As they moved through the record's five pieces, each one an indescribably deep musical conversation, Other Dimensions In Music provided example after perfect example of the deepest kind of bond between master musicians.

Throughout the album, there is never a unison melody line stated by the two horn players (Campbell on trumpet, and Carter on saxophones, flute, and occasionally trumpet as well); rather, they continually exchange short phrases and runs. When one solos, the other comments concisely on the ideas expressed. Solos quite often turn into duets, or into dances, the 'lead' instrument falling into line with the rumblings of the rhythm section for a few moments, then hurtling back into frenzied improvisation. Like the aforementioned Rob Brown disc, the music sounds like an expansion of the ideas Ornette Coleman proposed with his first quartet (Don Cherry, Charlie Haden, Billy Higgins and sometimes Ed Blackwell). This is particularly notable in the way melody rises out of Campbell's and Carter's exchanges, and the way Parker's bass underpins them. Parker doesn't bow the bass much with Other Dimensions In Music. He tends to play a more explicitly rhythmic role than with any of his other groups, allowing Campbell and Carter freer rein. This pays off tremendously, particularly on the above-mentioned epic opening cut of *Now!*; which, despite its half-hour, length never becomes boring. In fact, the listener is left at the end, wondering where the time went. The piece is an almost perfect crystallization of everything that free jazz is supposed to aspire to, captivating the listener with instantaneous creation and never resorting to cliché. Beginning with, as described above, Campbell and Carter playing off one another, "For The Glass Tear" winds its way through a series of variations on post-bop small group jazz. Campbell takes the first solo, heading, as he so often does, for the trumpet's higher range. After awhile, he is joined by Carter on alto sax, who then takes a lengthy solo of his own. Carter soon switches to flute, and begins a duet with William Parker—one of the few occasions when he bows the bass on the album. Rashid Bakr, who has been fairly active and hard-swinging throughout the piece thus far, lies back during the Carter/Parker duet, offering only the most subtle of cymbal accents.

Interestingly, "For The Glass Tear" is the only piece on *Now!* which does not end in a fade-out or an edit, hinting that the track might have been another extended workout. The second track, "Tears For The Boy Wonder (For Winston Marsalis)" (*sic*), is a perfect example. Only five-and-a-half minutes long on album, it begins with a short bass intro, then becomes another duet as Campbell's trumpet enters. It is immediately obvious why the piece is dedicated to Marsalis, whose technique owes much to New Orleans retro styles: Campbell is growling through a mute, in finest 1920s "trad" fashion. This continues for the first three minutes of the piece, until Daniel Carter makes his entrance. Carter, too, is playing trumpet, and the two players exchange melodies, quite beautifully, until the piece fades out. While "Tears For The Boy Wonder" works within the bluesy idiom Marsalis has attempted to claim as his own, the resultant sound is much more compelling and beautiful than almost anything he has offered the jazz public to date. The avant-gardists he disdains have, on this track, beaten him at his own game.

The 33-minute playing time of "For The Glass Tear (After Evening's Orange)" and the fadeouts on all *Now!*'s other tracks demonstrate something important about Other Dimensions In Music, which is their propensity to work at great length. In performance, a set will commonly consist of one, or perhaps two extended pieces, completely improvised on the spot. The flow of music throughout an hour-plus Other Dimensions set is seamless. Each solo essayed by a group member rises out of the music organically; there are no leaps forward into the spotlight, as with bop-rooted music. The whole quartet adjusts, on the spot, to cushion and accent each member's individualistic contribution. The group's second Aum Fidelity record, *Time Is Of The Essence; The Essence Is Beyond Time,* is a perfect demonstration of this concept. The other thing the group's third disc makes clear is the very tenuous nature of the bond between these four musicians, and how utterly it can be altered by the presence of a single outside personality.

Time Is Of The Essence; The Essence Is Beyond Time documents a performance at the Knitting Factory from December 1997. On that occasion, Other Dimensions In Music was joined by Matthew Shipp on piano. The performance took place twelve days before all the members of Other Dimensions, save drummer Rashid Bakr, were to join Shipp in the studio for the recording of his album *Strata* (discussed in Chapter Four). It was the third time Shipp had joined the group in performance. They would work together again, in early 1998 and on other occasions since. And although the record is brilliant, and the music on it is performed at an extraordinary level, it is very, very different from *Now!.*

Matthew Shipp's instrumental style is almost nothing like the music of Other Dimensions In Music. Where their improvisations flow naturally, each member rising up from the whole and then being reabsorbed like a whale breaking the surface of the ocean for a moment to spume, Shipp's piano playing is anything but smooth. It's about rough edges and sharp corners, about jarring the listener with competing and contradictory sounds. For much of the album, the thrill is not in hearing Matthew Shipp absorb himself into the shifting group endeavor that is Other Dimensions In Music. Rather, it is in hearing him struggle against their sound, like someone being swallowed by quicksand. This conflict provides a very interesting dilemma for bassist William Parker. On the one hand, his musical relationship with Shipp is soul-deep. Should he assist the pianist, bolstering his efforts to take the music to a clanging, angular place? Or should he remain the foundation of the quartet, and play the role he has always played within Other Dimensions? Frankly, it's Parker's struggle to reconcile the two sides of his music which makes the album so fascinating. For Other Dimensions In Music is not only a musical place where there is no piano, it is a place where a piano can only serve as a distraction and a disruption. Theirs is a chordless space, where each instrument is free to fly as far and as fast as its player chooses, and a pianist, even one as relentlessly inventive and questing as Matthew Shipp, can only serve as an anchor. *Time Is Of The Essence; The Essence Is Beyond Time* never resolves itself into placid quintet jazz. From beginning to end, it is a roiling, pointillistic snowball fight, each player hurling notes at the others, and though it is a tremendous performance, it displays an entirely different, much more combative aspect of the group than any other recording they've made. It's also one of Shipp's fiercest appearances on record, anywhere.

Perhaps the best way to analyze *Time Is Of The Essence* is alongside *Strata*. For on *Strata*, Shipp is clearly in control. The piece "Strata," in all its 14 sections, is his composition, and he has determined the instrumentation for each track. The album can almost be seen as Shipp's wresting of control from Other Dimensions to himself. Particularly symbolic is the absence of drummer Rashid Bakr. Without the rhythm section intact, William Parker's loyalties naturally revert to Shipp, and thus the session proceeds. Further, with no drum to keep time, the horns cannot extend themselves as far as they might like, for fear of losing themselves entirely to formless solipsism. So Campbell and Carter hew fairly close to Shipp's compositional notes. These two records (along with Shipp's *Pastoral Composure*) provide a very interesting portrait of the dynamics of the relationship between Roy Campbell and Matthew Shipp. For though each respects the other tremendously (Shipp often calls Campbell his favorite trumpeter), their aesthetics are very different. Where Shipp treats jazz tradition as something to return to only to prove that you can do it, Campbell is very much rooted in the tradition. Indeed, it's his hard-bop foundation which allows him to go as far out as he does. He remembers where he started, so he can always go back.

• Charles Gayle

VII • CHARLES GAYLE: TREMBLING BEFORE GOD

Listening to Charles Gayle play the saxophone is like having someone hurl a bucket of ice water in your face. The comparison's been made before, but that doesn't make it any less accurate. His music (both in tone and the sheer wall-rattling force with which he plays) takes the screaming harmonics and overblowing of players from the '60s like Pharaoh Sanders and Albert Ayler, and catapults the whole storm, still howling, into the present. What's more, the age gap between Gayle and the rest of the players on the current free jazz scene (most are in their 40s; Gayle is 61) makes him one of the few active players who can legitimately claim to be a contemporary of Ayler, Marion Brown, Frank Wright, and others.

Unfortunately, writing about Gayle is difficult. He's notoriously hermetic, keeping a safe distance between himself and the rest of the New York musicians, to say nothing of his legendary caginess with the press. He doesn't work with the same players as everybody else, preferring to assemble his own bands using less well-known names, and often changing bands from album to album. (Drummer Michael Wimberley is one of the few musicians to appear with Gayle on any kind of regular basis.) Omnipresent scene bassist William Parker appears on a half-dozen of Gayle's recordings, notably *Kingdom Come, More Live* and *Touchin' On Trane,* but no other players covered in this book have worked with him to any serious extent.

Beyond his musical iconoclasm, though, Gayle prefers to live outside the spotlight. He shows up and performs, then disappears until the next gig. He lives a quiet, solitary life, and little is known about his past. He seemed, in fact, to have rocketed from the core of the Earth when he first achieved avant-jazz prominence in 1988, with a trio of albums—*Always Born, Homeless,* and *Spirits Before*—recorded in a single week and released by the Swedish label Silkheart. The only thing anyone (outside the very heart of the scene) knew about him then was the very thing he's most reluctant to discuss: his years of homelessness. The title of Gayle's second Silkheart album, *Homeless,* was a literal description. He spent between twelve and twenty years living on Manhattan's streets. (He's understandably shy about details and dates.) It's not even known whether this was a result of financial misfortune or of some prophet-wandering-in-the-wilderness impulse. The assumption would be that no one voluntarily takes on street life, but in our conversation, Gayle dropped hints about how he willingly gave away his possessions in the early 1970s. It's entirely possible that he went on a sort of spiritual pilgrimage, and that living on a sidewalk was a major component of that.

Gayle performed music in those years—not in clubs, but on the sidewalks and in the subways, for change. He's spoken in the past of only earning enough to eat once per day. Few other concrete facts about this period of Gayle's life emerge in conversation, but a fascinating story glimmers just out of reach, as he talks about having to fight off attacks and survive bitterly cold winter nights without any source of heat. Until he tells his story, nobody will know the whole truth about what Charles Gayle's life was like before his emergence onto the jazz scene. Yet from that point on, he has been an undeniable and nearly ubiquitous presence on the Downtown scene. He was, early on and to the present day, a great beneficiary of Michael Dorf's patronage. Dorf, the owner of the Knitting Factory, gave Gayle a stage on which to perform, and signed him to a record contract. Gayle played weeklong stands at the Knitting Factory, and has released the vast majority of his albums through Knitting Factory Records, including *Kingdom Come* and *Ancient Of Days,* which are among his best work. He's also recorded for FMP, Black Saint, Blast

First, Audible Hiss, and 2.13.61. And, in addition to his Knitting Factory performances (which cemented the lore surrounding him in New York), has performed at Tonic and the Vision Festival. At one point, he undertook a lengthy residency at the Cooler, a former meatpacking warehouse turned (literally) underground music venue.

Talking to Gayle in person is a pleasure, despite his somewhat diffident nature, and it's easy to see where he gets the stamina and lung-power for his extended, ranting musical workouts. Sitting in his tiny Manhattan apartment, he can spiel for hours, pausing only occasionally to lapse into thought before making his next statement. He's evasive and open at the same time—he'll talk at length about issues of record company politics, social history, or Christianity (the latter being a topic which plays a significant, although not dominant, role in his music). Yet, there are certain areas a conversation simply will not be allowed to venture into, and those boundaries are strictly enforced. At the same time, there is Gayle's relative egolessness, and near-continual self-abnegation, to contend with. Every sentence seems bracketed by disclaimers. When we spoke, he was quite firm about not wishing to be recorded, and more importantly, about not having a fuss made over him in the pages of this book. He kept using words like "irrelevant" to describe himself, his music, and his contributions to the New York free jazz scene.

Despite his modesty, it's hard to underemphasize the importance of Gayle's musical output. The fact is that, if one asks someone who knows relatively little about free jazz what a "free jazz" saxophonist sounds like, the description they give will likely be more similar to Charles Gayle's work than anyone else's. Some might say that this implies Gayle's work is clichéd. I believe the opposite is true; I believe Gayle may well be the archetypal free jazz player, as well as being the last man standing from the revolutionary explosions taking place in the music in the 1960s. Albert Ayler is dead. John Coltrane is dead. Pharoah Sanders has mellowed substantially, and now makes world-music albums with Bill Laswell. The only players left from the first generation who retain the sheer lung-power of the vanished greats are Charles Gayle and Arthur Doyle, and Doyle is Gayle's musical inferior by a long stretch. For example, listen to *Illuminators* (Audible Hiss), Gayle's duo album with drummer Sunny Murray, and then to *Dawn Of A New Vibration* (Fractal), Doyle's album of duos with Murray. While the Doyle album has moments of nerve-jangling power, the saxophonist runs short of ideas at quite a few points during the recording, leaving the brilliant drummer to bolster the music and keep it moving. Gayle's performance on *Illuminators* suffers no such flaws. Beginning on piano, then moving to saxophone, he battles with Murray for every inch of space from the first note to the last; it's a captivating record, and should be in every Gayle fan's collection.

In addition to playing tenor saxophone and piano, Gayle plays bass clarinet, violin, and drums. He claims to be entirely self-taught on all of these instruments, save for piano lessons in childhood. During our nearly three-hour conversation, he did not cite any major influences on his playing, for any of his instruments, though he expressed admiration for John Coltrane, Cecil Taylor (with whom he's played), Albert Ayler and Sun Ra at various points. Interestingly, Gayle's style on each of these instruments is very different from the others. When he plays the tenor saxophone, the instrument for which he has become most famous, he's a one-man hurricane, blasting overtones and screeches based around nothing more than instantaneous inspiration. His playing is totally improvised; his compositions are given religious or spiritual titles ("Repent," "Holy Faith," "Hymn Of Redemption") after the fact. Rather than use screams or overblowing as climactic gestures, he often uses them as starting points, and continues to climb up and out from there. He often reaches vistas of sonic terror from which even a hell-jazz warrior like Peter Brötzmann might quail.

On piano, by contrast, Gayle is a much more contemplative player. I saw him perform a solo piano show a few days after Thanksgiving, 2000, at Tonic. The room contained perhaps three dozen people. Gayle wasn't worried about them. He sat with his head tilted at an oblique angle to the keyboard, following the movements of his hands with his eyes. He barely paused to acknowledge applause at the end of one piece, before moving quickly into the next. The music he performed was an odd mix of New Orleans stride boogie, slow blues, and free outbursts. During a set which lasted just over an hour, Gayle played a half-dozen pieces. I recognized two; one was based on the melody of the standard "Softly As In A Morning Sunrise," and the other was a Thelonious Monk composition which I knew, but couldn't name.

"Softly As In A Morning Sunrise" has been one of my favorite standards since I heard John Coltrane perform it on *Live At The Village Vanguard*. Sonny Rollins' version, from his own *An Evening At The Village Vanguard* album, is also superb. Gayle's interpretation of the tune, on piano, couldn't have been more different from the two saxophonists' renditions (even discounting the shock of hearing Gayle perform standards at all). He approached the melody infrequently and tentatively, offering one quick run-through of the song's sinuous main line, barely completing it before leaping back into formless improvisation.

The other pieces Gayle performed that night were, like the two standards, melodic at their core. He often reverted to basic blues and boogie-woogie riffs, ascending from these into quick flurries of free playing but always returning to the simplistic, almost New Orleans-style lines which formed the foundation of each number. At times the disjunction between the free and structured portions of the pieces became rather schizophrenic, the wilder sections sounding less like a natural outgrowth of what he'd been playing a moment before and more like an outburst, a sudden spike on a relatively calm EEG.

This difference between Gayle's piano and saxophone styles is just one of the things which make him a fascinating performer—in some ways, the most fascinating performer on the New York scene. Part of it is a kind of silent wonder as this tall, thin, soft-spoken and seemingly frail man conjures a music that sounds like it could rip holes in the sky and earth. And Gayle's onstage manner is as captivating as his music. When actually playing, he tends to shut down, focusing on the music and not acknowledging applause or any kind of crowd response until the end of the set. (When I saw his solo piano performance, he spent about five minutes, after he finished playing, apologizing for not bringing his saxophone and explaining that he and the horn were "not getting along these days.") Since his performances are totally improvised (while he does occasionally play recognizable songs, he doesn't plan which songs he's going to play), it's not surprising that he would concentrate onstage to the point of being oblivious to the crowd. However, Gayle's shows can become the most interesting when he's not making music at all—there are other aspects to his life, and career, which induce the kind of fear mixed with excitement that can only come from watching someone skirt closer and closer to the edge of madness.

Gayle is a man of passionate religious belief. This is obvious from the most cursory glance at his discography. Albums bear titles like *Delivered, Repent, Raining Fire* and *Daily Bread.* Individual tracks are called "Yes, God Is Real," "Sanctification" or "Redeemed." He's also passionately pro-life. This latter conviction emerges in his performances, sometimes to controversial, and even disastrous, effect. There is a tape available which contains a five-minute excerpt from a performance during which Gayle abandoned music entirely in favor of a 25-minute harangue about abortion and sexual politics. Gayle admits his attitudes and beliefs, and the onstage behavior those beliefs sometimes engender, have cost him bookings. Nevertheless, he feels that expressing his feelings on the subject is more important than playing music for a living. In fact, there are times when he has abandoned music, showing up for bookings in an entirely different guise.

Gayle occasionally performs in pantomime. Painting the lower half of his face in vertical white stripes, wearing a red clown nose, a bowler hat, black jacket and white gloves, he appears at some of his shows in the guise of "Streets," a character he created. Tooting on a small, plastic toy trumpet, or plinking a tiny piano, "Streets" acts out psychodramas which explain Gayle's views on social issues. This aspect of his career has, in the past, proved even more controversial (and—to some writers—infuriating) than his rants from the stage. One infamous "Streets" performance, on the subject of abortion, caused a sizable outcry. Gayle, with bloodstained arms, approached audience members holding plastic baby dolls and surgical implements, offering these grisly props to the horrified onlookers as if to ask them to "abort" the toy fetuses. Gayle hasn't been invited back to that performance space. Perhaps he realizes that there's only so much controversy audiences will tolerate; "Streets" has not put in any appearances of late, though the cover of Gayle's most recent album, *Ancient Of Days,* is a painting which depicts everyone on the sidewalk wearing "Streets"-like facial makeup and hats.

Ancient Of Days is an important item in Gayle's discography; it represents something of a break in his usual totally-improvised style, and a triumphant leap forward for his music. On the CD, Gayle and a trio (pianist Hank Johnson, bassist Juini Booth and drummer Michael Wimberley) bring the music back down to earth. They also rein it in somewhat; the longest cut on the disc is "only" 16 minutes, and in the process, the four discover a beauty and a sense of artistic centeredness that was sometimes absent from earlier releases.

The tracks have the sense of being at least minimally composed; on the opening cut, "Betrayal," Gayle continues to search out every sonic possibility available to the tenor saxophone, but behind him Booth and Johnson maintain a steady blues walk, punctuated by Wimberley's snapping snare drum. Wimberley has long been Gayle's secret weapon, but on this disc he truly comes into his own. He's not a flashy power drummer like Sunny Murray, or a skittering polyrhythmist like Rashied Ali (both of whom Gayle's worked with in the past); instead, his minimalism provides a counterpoint to, and a foundation for, Gayle's expansive, harrowing explorations.

When a drum solo finally arrives, it's a pointillistic revelation, not a foregone conclusion.

Juini Booth's bass playing is also beautifully showcased here; his bowing in particular creates a haunted atmosphere not often found on Gayle's other, more bombastic releases. *Ancient Of Days* takes Gayle's interpretation of the '60s free tradition and, by refining its blues tinges, makes it all the more powerful. It's one of his best records to date.

It's also one of the few genuinely satisfying records he's made with an outside pianist. Gayle prefers to work in trio form, with a few duo and solo discs also available. When he goes outside the saxophone-bass-drums format, it's often to add an additional string player, as on *Daily Bread* (where he's joined by Wilber Morris on bass, and William Parker, playing cello) or the two-CD set *More Live* (where, again, he has two stringed instruments backing him). On *Daily Bread*, Gayle also plays violin on two tracks, "Our Sins" and "Offering To Christ." (On "Our Sins," drummer Wimberly plays violin, Wilber Morris plays bass, and Parker plays cello. On "Offering To Christ," the instrumentation is Morris on bass, Wimberly on violin, Gayle on violin, and Parker on piano.) The only major album, other than *Ancient Of Days*, on which Gayle is backed by a piano trio is 1997's *Delivered*, released through 2.13.61. *Delivered* is, even in Gayle's judgment, a relatively unsuccessful record. During our talk, he explained that he was having trouble with his saxophone that day, and couldn't get the sound he wanted, which is why the record sounds as tentative and timid as it does. A collection of pieces written in gospel style, it never goes out far enough to allow any genuine expression on the bandmembers' parts; it's the only Gayle album I've ever heard which could be described as boring or forgettable.

Though it brought him some slight rock-scene recognition, Gayle's association with Rollins (the owner of 2.13.61) could certainly be deemed an artistic non-starter. *Delivered* was the only record Gayle released on 2.13.61, and it's one of his least-known albums. At some point in the mid-'90s, he recorded an album of instrumental jams with the Rollins Band, but both he and the band decided that the material was lackluster, and wouldn't reflect well on anyone involved, so it was never released. Somewhat more successfully, Gayle, along with drummer Rashied Ali, provided musical backing for the audiobook version of *Everything,* a section of Rollins' book *Eye Scream.* Gayle's work (on piano and saxophone) on that disc got favorable reviews. Rollins and Gayle remain admirers of each other's work, but they no longer do business together.

Unlike David S. Ware and Matthew Shipp—who have become virtual ambassadors from jazz to alt-rock and back—the further away Charles Gayle stays, it seems, the better his music is. Indeed, two of his greatest albums find him delving deep into the free jazz tradition, and playing with two of its most legendary drummers.

On 1993's *Touchin' On Trane* (FMP), Gayle recorded two days' worth of blistering material with William Parker and Rashied Ali. Ali was John Coltrane's drummer during the last years of the saxophonist's life. He performed on Coltrane's most extreme and least compromising albums, most notably *Meditations,* the 4-CD *Live In Japan* set (released posthumously, and featuring hour-long versions of Coltrane classics like "Crescent" and "My Favorite Things"), and particularly *Interstellar Space,* an album of saxophone-drums duets which can give the impression of not only rocketing through space, but being bombarded by meteors while doing so. By performing with Ali, Gayle links himself firmly to free jazz's past, and through his playing, takes it into the future.

Touchin' On Trane is one of the few albums to win acclaim outside the relatively small circle of listeners who customarily embrace free jazz records. *The Penguin Guide To Jazz On CD* awards it four stars and a crown, the book's highest honor, and the editors describe it thusly in their review: "The outright masterpiece [of Gayle's discography] is the FMP album, which seems likely to be a central document in the free music of the decade: the three men touch on Coltrane from moment to moment (and Ali renews his old relationship in triumph) but this is new, brilliant, eloquent free playing." The album is worthy of such fulsome praise; if a listener were to buy only one Gayle disc, *Touchin' On Trane* should be the one.

The disc consists of five tracks, simply titled "Part A" through "Part E," which vary from just under five to nearly 28 minutes in length. Recorded on Halloween and All Saints' Day 1991, though not released until 1993, the album is notable for the ways in which Gayle's playing differs from any other session in his discography. Avoiding his usual long screams, the saxophonist plays in an almost post-bop style, releasing streams of notes in time with Ali's relentless, full-speed-ahead drumming and Parker's throbbing bass. Ali is a fascinating drummer, and it's quite clearly his work which altered the dynamics of the trio. Never a power hitter like his contemporaries Ronald Shannon Jackson and Sunny Murray, Ali dwells on washes of cymbals and other "pulse" effects throughout the *Touchin' On Trane* album. This was his greatest contribution to free jazz drumming in the 1960s—the idea of playing "pulse" rhythms, which did not keep strict time but rather kept the drums underneath the music as a constant, shifting undercurrent, bolstering the music but allowing it to roam freely without being pushed in one direction or another by the bass and snare, or the demands of "swing." This style allows a great deal more interaction between the drummer and the lead instrument(s), outside of the traditional call-and-response of swing-based playing. This was proved most strongly by Ali on *Interstellar Space,* but a number of other saxophone-drum duo CDs (discussed elsewhere in this book) show that the concept has definitely taken hold, and provided much room for brilliant, introspective work.

Of all the tracks on *Touchin' On Trane,* the one which comes closest to realizing the artistic claims of the title is "Part B." A slow, mournful piece, it finds Gayle taking a particularly Coltrane-esque approach to his horn. Latching onto a hint of melody, he worries at the phrase repeatedly, exploring it in all its possible permutations for nearly seven minutes. Behind him, Parker bows the bass, creating a haunting counter-melody which shifts constantly, to accommodate Gayle's improvisational flights. Ali, for his part, keeps the drums at a steady whisper at the very bottom of the music, never explicitly commenting on anything but always standing ready to offer support. It's a suspenseful, time-stopping piece of music, and one of the highlights of a truly amazing record.

Kingdom Come, from 1994, is a very different sort of album. It features two solo piano performances, but again, it's primarily a trio disc, recorded partly live, and partly in the studio. William Parker is, again, the bassist of choice, but the drummer is Sunny Murray, best known for his work with Cecil Taylor and Albert Ayler in the mid-1960s. *Kingdom Come* opens with "Seven Days," one of the two piano solos ("Redeemed," the fifth track, is the other), but the second cut, "Lord Lord," is the centerpiece of the album, and one of Gayle's most shattering performances on record. A live saxophone-bass-drums workout, it lasts nearly 22 minutes, and all three players are at full force throughout. Parker bows underneath as the piece begins, creating a furious, sawing effect on the instrument. Gayle soars from the first note, letting loose long, honking screams with little regard for cleanliness of tone or any kind of structure at all. This is a pure "energy music" performance, the equal of anything by Ayler, Sanders or Coltrane.

Murray, like Ali was on *Touchin' On Trane,* is the catalyst for the album's mood here, and his style of playing couldn't be more different from the other man's. Therefore, the two Gayle performances are totally divergent from one another, to the point of seeming like the work of two different players at times. Murray is as fond of the cymbals as Ali, but he has none of Ali's tentative touch; he's much more interested in creating crashes, like tidal waves sweeping away seaside hotels. Murray assaults his drums with the same force Gayle brings to the saxophone, and the throbbing, pounding power of his playing makes it seem sometimes as though two or three drummers are back there, each with his own kit. Tremendous bashes of the snare and toms accompany Gayle's high-flying outbursts and cries of mingled ecstasy and torment, while Parker bows out a melody which never attempts to provide anything like a guide, or an indication of where the ensemble will head; instead, the bassist creates a third solo voice. The listener, when first encountering "Holy Holy," has the same reaction as he might to Cecil Taylor's *Nefertiti, The Beautiful One Has Come* (discussed in Chapter Two); it's impossible to reconcile the three seemingly separate strands of music playing at once, and the only choice is to pick one and focus on it. Only later, upon repeated playing, does any kind of unity begin to present itself, and the beauty of the work as a whole emerge.

You might say that the reaction an unprepared jazz listener will have to Charles Gayle's music is similar to that of a religious conversion. Not the sort of conversion which happens through study and debate, and eventual intellectual embrace of the tenets and concepts of a particular faith, but rather the sort of conversion that overtook Saul of Tarsus, who was (according to the Christian Bible) struck from his horse by the force of God, and rose up a Christian. It's reasonable to assume that Gayle—between his album and track titles and the sheer Old Testament fury of his playing— wants to convert people with a music whose effect is similar to the total-immersion conversion-dunkings practiced by Southern Baptists. The listener emerges from a Gayle performance spluttering, catching his breath, and half-wondering what just happened. Only later, with reflection, does the profound effect of this man's saxophone on the heart and mind become clear. And at that point, there's no going back. People who have embraced Charles Gayle's music stick with it; no one responds "Yeah, that was all right, I guess." It's all or nothing, on his part and his audience's.

• Joe Morris

VIII • JOE MORRIS: KEEPIN' IT CLEAN

I didn't get Joe Morris when I first heard his music. While I enjoyed his playing immediately, I didn't understand exactly where he was going. Sure, there was something about it that got my attention—he was the first jazz guitarist, other than Sonny Sharrock, whose work leaped forward and seemed like more than just accompaniment—but I couldn't get a handle on what I was hearing. His note choices seemed obscure. I didn't know why he chose to play what he did. Somehow, for all the (undeniable) beauty of his playing, there was still a distance between me and the music. Morris' records, even the ones which were totally improvised, didn't seem to have the lapel-gripping immediacy of, say, Charles Gayle or Other Dimensions In Music. And since I wasn't yanked into it with my heart and guts, I began to intellectualize the music and listen to it that way, the way I'd listen to a classical string quartet or a piece of experimental electronic music. I viewed Morris' cleanly articulated, melodic beauty as cool, withdrawn from the moment. It wasn't until I saw him onstage that it all came together for me. And I realized how completely I'd misinterpreted him.

I saw Morris perform with a trio (Timo Stanko on bass and Jerome Deupree—formerly of Morphine—on drums) at Tonic. Also on the bill was Morris' frequent collaborator, Mat Maneri, though the two did not play together this time. The Joe Morris Trio represents Morris' relaxed, yet focused, attitude perfectly in its music. The primary dynamic within the group is the relationship between Morris and Jerome Deupree, who have been playing together for about fifteen years now. Deupree appears on Morris' first (self-released) CD, *Sweatshop,* from 1990, and has remained with the Trio since then. (The Joe Morris Quartet, in which Mat Maneri plays, has had various drummers, including Deupree and Curt Newton, but Gerald Cleaver's the man behind the kit as of this writing.) Bassist Timo Stanko is younger than Morris and Deupree, and is a relative newcomer to the Trio. Nevertheless, his skill and sense of innovation on the upright bass have marked him as a nearly ideal addition to the group. At the Tonic gig, he took two solos in a 45-minute set, each of which was fully engaging and impressive, particularly the second. During this performance, he strummed and slapped the strings with extraordinary speed and force, making the bass sound like a huge guitar. Deupree followed him for a few moments, accenting his throbs and rumbles with quick fills and rustling cymbals, but eventually Timo was on his own, and he held the crowd utterly captive while he explored every option available to him, all without ever losing the innate rhythm of the piece. When he finished his solo, and brought the group back together for the conclusion of the piece, the audience erupted in joy and appreciation.

It was Morris' lead work, though, that was the greatest revelation to me. As stated above, I'd always enjoyed his music, but in an abstract, almost theoretical way. His pure, clean tone, and his note choices, tended to remind me of European-style "free music" more than full-throttle jazz. Though it was never boring, there was always something missing for me. The *sound* of his guitar made his playing a little too easy to ignore, to tune out, on a CD.

Onstage, the opposite was true. Morris took command of the room, the band, and the audience in a way I'd never seen before. His tone hadn't changed in the slightest from the records; he still wasn't using any kind of distortion or electronic effects. There was nothing there but the sound of a guitar played through an amplifier. But the music, in that space, with a rapt audience in front of him, took on a physicality, an irresistible force, I'd never felt listening to the albums. There was no distancing effect, like I'd gotten from the records; Morris was going for total mental, physical and spiritual engagement with the audience. Without the constraints of the recording studio (an environment which can often prove sterile, and creatively limiting), the music took on a kind of fervor it had never had for me before. Morris led the band through composed themes and improvised workouts, but the common denominator was not abstraction; it was swing. Not in some Brian Setzer Orchestra way, but the way a primo piano trio—Bud Powell, Ray Brown and Max Roach, say—swings. These three musicians were swinging *hard*, particularly Morris and Deupree, who seemed to be almost competing with one another to see who could summon the greatest rhythmic power and impetus behind their playing. The guitar solos rippled out into the air and demanded attention. Somehow, in the live context, the same qualities that had seemed innocuous and easily dismissed, when harnessed to the pure swinging energy of the rhythm section, became incredibly powerful stylistic gestures, and proved impossible to ignore.

The 45-minute set was one of the best evenings of music I'd witnessed all year. When I watched Morris' trio perform, I heard what I'd been missing in his music—watching him do it made his methods, and his goals, clear to me in a way the discs had not. But afterward, the records took on an additional dimension for me. I was able to hear *more* there than I had been before. When I listen to the CDs now, in light of having seen Morris and his trio at full capacity, I can fully appreciate them. So, although Joe Morris' albums contain some of the most brilliant jazz guitar playing on the planet, don't pass up a chance to see him live, because the performance is crucial to his aesthetic and methodology. As it should be—as it always is—in the best jazz.

Morris' commitment to a clean tone is one of the most important factors in his work. "My music's always been clean," he told me when we spoke. "My playing's always been clean. I made a very serious effort to not be Sonny Sharrock. I never wanted to be a thrash kind of free jazz guitarist in that sense. I find that that's very lazy. Not Sonny Sharrock, Sonny Sharrock is fine. I know he was breaking his ground the way he had to do it, and he's a different person. But he has a space. So I never wanted to invade his space. I'm very sure about that all the time. I also never wanted to invade Derek Bailey's space. Or Blood Ulmer's space."

The three musicians Morris cites are probably the three most important jazz guitarists of the post-bop era (roughly, 1968 to the present). Sharrock was the one to depart in the most obvious way from jazz guitar tradition, bringing a heavily distorted sound—reminiscent of Jimi Hendrix—to the jazz group format. He made a few crucial recordings in the 1960s, appearing on Pharaoh Sanders' *Tauhid* and his own *Black Woman* with wife Linda, but then dropped out of sight until the mid-1980s, when he was rediscovered by bassist/producer Bill Laswell. Sharrock and Laswell worked together on solo albums for Sharrock (*Guitar* and *Ask The Ages*—the latter being a reunion with Pharaoh Sanders—are the keepers), as well as in the astonishingly noisy improv quartet Last Exit with saxophonist Peter Brötzmann and drummer Ronald Shannon Jackson.

British iconoclast Derek Bailey, by contrast, is often interested in microscopic gestures. Creating an almost entirely new musical style and a highly individual sound, he has attempted to turn his back on basically every preconceived notion of guitar playing, with debatable success. While he has a substantial cult following, his music can seem almost autistic to a first-time listener. Only when collaborators attempt to drag him out of his self-imposed exile does any truly exciting music result (his duo CD with Japanese guitarist Keiji Haino is one such example, as are his recordings with Japanese bass-drums duo Ruins).

James "Blood" Ulmer has had a somewhat schizophrenic career. He plays brilliantly when he wants to, adapting Ornette Coleman's melodic and rhythmic concepts to guitar-based funk-jazz in truly exciting ways. On too many sessions, though, he seems to be just going through the motions: playing washed-out, rudimentary blues and funk, and cutting loose with some of the most unkempt vocalizing to be found in any music since Captain Beefheart. His

VIII • JOE MORRIS: KEEPIN' IT CLEAN

records are almost always a gamble, with the exception of *Are You Glad To Be In America?*, *Tales Of Captain Black* and his recordings with the Odyssey trio (guitar, violin and drums).

Each of these three players, whatever anybody thinks of their music, has had an undeniable impact on jazz guitar, and Morris is keenly aware of his position relative to theirs. "Those three guys are dealing with criteria that end up determining what the technique of the music is," he told me. "So if you don't get close to dealing with some of these things, then you're functioning in a kind of archaic vacuum. There are thresholds that you have to contend with, and what you have to do is deal with those and still come out as yourself. I'm really serious about that. Part of the reason I have that specific kind of intent and rhetoric for it is because I'm really probably more influenced by the aesthetics of the AACM [Association for the Advancement of Creative Music—a Chicago-based arts collective which spawned the Art Ensemble Of Chicago, among other bands and projects] and Cecil Taylor than I am by Albert Ayler or New Thing free jazz. So the precision in my music is based on the sense that I needed to do something else [other than over-the-top wailing], and precision was very important. As far as tone, I always want to have my sound be as clear as I can get it, so it doesn't sound like I'm playing rock guitar. I don't like distortion on my guitar. I like it clean, so that the lines—I think the line is the point. And in that sense, you know, I kinda think that if I'd done any of those things [adopting a style with more rock-audience appeal], I would've been a lot more popular. But I wouldn't have been playing what I wanted to play. I never wanted to merge 'electric guitar' into the jazz thing. I just wanted to play the language of the music on the guitar. I'm just using the place that we've arrived at, and putting it on the guitar. The same way Lonnie Johnson did with Louis Armstrong, or Barney Kessel did with Lester Young. Just try to put the most current language of the music on my instrument, and not concern myself with it being successful. I don't have any control over that. I try not to fail, but I can tell you that that's been my problem all along."

The relative prettiness of Morris' playing isn't the only thing which conflicts with potential listeners' preconceptions of what a "free jazz guitarist" should be playing—there's also the aforementioned desire to have the music *swing*. "I have the audacity to try to articulate swing on my instrument," Morris said to me, "and therefore there's a whole group of people who might like me, who won't like me because I'm articulating swing. Even though I think articulating swing is the absolute most radical thing I can do. It's the most uncommercial thing I can possibly do. Playing noise guitar has a commercial element to it. It always has. It's always been done by people who cannot understand what I'm talking about when I talk about the swing thing, so I separate them from my aesthetic. They're different from my aesthetic. I'm interested in Blood Ulmer, Grant Green, Wes Montgomery, Bern Nix. I like some of the European guys, but I don't feel a similar aesthetic connection to them, although there are some things they do that I feel informs us at this point. For years everyone told me I should play like [Derek Bailey] if I wanted to be successful, and I said, what's the point of that? There's lots of people I could play like and be a lot more successful. I can play the guitar. I could play like anybody. You want me to be successful, I'm gonna pick the guy that is the strangest thing?" At the same time, though, Morris is not discounting the musical contributions of the noisier avant-garde guitarists. "I'm not the type of person to say 'That's not guitar playing,' because, you know, I'm not that stupid. It's just, it expresses a different thing. When music is judged on aesthetic terms, rather than 'Well, that's not guitar playing' or 'That's experimental'—I hate the word experimental. I hate that. Because no one is making music without an aesthetic subtext, and they're not saying 'Let me try this, and see if it works.' Works how? That it gets popular? Is that the experiment? As a creative act, music is the expression of an aesthetic. My aesthetic is really detailed, and very consistent. I'm trying to be part of the African-American jazz continuum. That's it. I'm not trying to be a 'new music' guitar player. I'm trying to be a jazz guitar player. A new jazz guitar player. That's all I ever wanted to be. That's what I am. And I've had to defend that to people. Which I think is a great luxury. I feel like I did it. Because I achieved what I strive for, which is to make something that doesn't pander in any way."

Just because Morris' music doesn't pander to the listener doesn't mean it's not enjoyable on a visceral level—he's hardly dwelling exclusively in the realm of rarefied intellectualism. His first CD, *Sweatshop* (an earlier vinyl-only album, *Wraparound,* may be reissued on disc by Atavistic Records as part of the Unheard Music series), is a collection of funk-based themes; it finds him backed by Jerome Deupree on drums and Sebastian Steinberg, a frequent early collaborator, on electric bass. The music is nowhere near the static realm of much jazz-funk, and Morris' insistent avoidance of electronic trickery keeps it from being overly rockist. The end result is a disc which is clearly informed by, if not indebted to, Ornette Coleman's work with his electric band Prime Time, not to mention the angular, excoriating work of the late-1970s British post-punk quartet Gang Of Four. Deupree hits the kit harder than anywhere else in Morris' discography on *Sweatshop,* and this spurs Morris to heights of emotionalism reminiscent of Funkadelic guitarist Eddie Hazel or Catfish Collins (brother of legendary bassist Bootsy Collins), the former lead guitarist of James Brown's JBs. In fact, "Four Pests," the opening stomp on *Sweatshop,* sounds like nothing so much as a free-funk reworking of Catfish Collins' awe-inspiring solo on "Ain't It Funky Now," from the James Brown live album *Love Power Peace—Live At The Olympia, Paris, 1971.* Collins, like Morris, eschewed any sort of feedback or distortion on his guitar, and worked primarily within the 'chicken picking' style of R&B instrumentals. This style, with its high-speed runs of tightly constricted notes, is a major stylistic underpinning of *Sweatshop,* and makes it one of the biggest surprises in Morris' catalog.

The more aggressive side of Morris expressed on *Sweatshop* couldn't be further from the music he produces with his Quartet, and particularly in collaboration with violinist Mat Maneri (one of the only steady members of the Quartet, whose bass and drum chairs rotate fairly often). The Joe Morris Quartet has released four CDs to date—*You Be Me* (Soul Note, 1997); *Underthru* (OmniTone, 1999); *A Cloud Of Black Birds* (Aum Fidelity, 1999); and *At The Old Office* (Knitting Factory, 2000). Each of these records differs slightly, but the factor common to all of them is their continuing exploration of the relationship between Morris and Maneri (which has most recently been taken to its logical extreme with a duo CD, *Soul Search,* on Aum Fidelity).

Once again, the cleanliness of Morris' tone is of primary importance to the music. Because his lack of effects limits the length to which he can hold a note (he doesn't even use a whammy bar), his music always retains a certain jaggedness, his notes often emerging in staccato bursts. This is contrasted quite ably, within the Quartet, by Maneri's violin. The violin's ability to offer both high-speed runs of short notes, and long drones, allows Maneri to leap over Morris sometimes, and underpin him other times, creating a continuous conversation while the bassist and drummer (on *You Be Me,* Nate McBride and Curt Newton; on *A Cloud Of Black Birds,* Chris Lightcap and Jerome Deupree; and on *Underthru* and *At The Old Office,* Lightcap and Gerald Cleaver) keep the ensemble moving forward steadily and as a constantly cohesive unit. The music of the Quartet is much smoother than the music of the Trio, even though Morris' style remains defiantly individualistic, and doesn't reshape itself much from one configuration to the other. It's easy to hear that Maneri's swooping and hovering violin lines draw the music much closer to an Elliott Carter-esque chamber music sound, than to a more traditionally jazz-rooted exploration of the guitar-bass-drums trio.

Another definite difference between the Trio and the Quartet is the shape and sound of the notes, and this is again attributable to Maneri. Morris told me "Within the context that I described about being a particular kind of guitar player, basically trying to be an extension of the jazz tradition, to take that as a language...there are different dialects that are spoken. And sometimes new ones emerge. The way Mat Maneri improvises has some very unique characteristics that pose a challenge to me as a guitar player. He uses microtonal phrasing and intervals, plays very slowly sometimes, he has an incredible way of using atonality that's very fluid." The easiest way to explain microtones to a non-musician is, they're the notes between the notes on the traditional Western scale. Western notation was developed for use in orchestras—with it, everyone tunes to the same pitch, and plays together harmoniously. But in the music of other nations, particularly India and Asian countries, tones which fall between the standard Western pitches are employed, allowing musicians to create resonant drones (think of the contrast between a harmonium and a sitar in classical Indian music). Maneri adapts this technique to the violin, creating an almost hypnotic effect by playing notes that seem just on the edge of those the Western ear is familiar with. Listening to him, you often find yourself tilting your head to the side like a dog, trying to figure out whether he's playing something really weird, or you're just hearing it wrong. The effect, of hearing new tones from an instrument that by all rights should have exhausted its possibilities for novelty after several hundred years, is fascinating. Morris isn't Maneri's only admirer—Matthew Shipp considers him one of the musicians who will be absolutely crucial to jazz's future. His recent quartet album, *Blue Decco* (Thirsty Ear), provides a lot of supporting evidence. Recorded with Craig Taborn on piano, William Parker on bass, and Gerald Cleaver on drums, the disc is a swinging, but slightly off-center, collection of eight tunes, including the Matthew Shipp composition "The New Lord's Prayer" and Duke Ellington's "I Got It Bad."

But Maneri's hypnotic tone isn't the only thing that attracted Morris to the violinist. "He has a very strong rhythmic flow," Morris continued, "and a very strong melodic flow, and a really unique way of putting an outer layer of material on it. So it poses a challenge to play with somebody like him. It gives me a chance to add some new material to my guitar technique. Because that's one of the things you do in this kind of world. I'm creating technique for the guitar. The way I play guitar is incredibly difficult. I don't make a big deal about that, but I can tell you when people come to take a lesson with me and they think that they don't have it, it's very hard to do. And it's really hard to do consistently. But I always want to make it more. It's okay [in jazz] to be technical. Charlie Parker's the greatest saxophonist that ever lived, and that's fine, but everybody wants to be better than him. They want to be able to play more than Charlie Parker. And if they can't play more, they want to play something he never played. Or exploit one aspect of what he played. Dealing with technique is a big thing. Rather than looking for a very strong visceral experience, you enjoy the details, and there's viscera within that. Subtlety, melody—melody is an amazing, powerful force. And when it gets inside people's heads, it really does a lot to them. Swing and rhythm are also really, really powerful, and when they get inside people's bodies, they have a very powerful effect on them. So I'd say I play with Mat because he has his own technique, and he forces me to expand mine."

The questions of technique, melody, and subtlety came up again and again in my conversation with Morris. As a guitarist, he has two sets of preconceptions bouncing him back and forth. First, there is the idea of the "jazz guitarist," a subtle, chord-playing accompanist like Wes Montgomery or Grant Green, providing a slight additional foundation, alongside the pianist, for the explorations of the more "traditional" instruments (typically trumpet or saxophone). Morris has found himself in this circumstance in the past, somewhat against his will. Most recently, this happened on the Whit Dickey Quartet album *Big Top* (Wobbly Rail, 2000). Although Morris' playing is brilliant throughout the four-track disc, which includes versions of Eric Dolphy's "The Prophet" and Thelonious Monk's "Skippy," he is often relegated to a sideman's role with a low place in the soundmix, directly opposite bassist Chris Lightcap, while pride of place is given to saxophonist Rob Brown. This is not to take anything away from the album as a piece of music; all four men are close friends who

VIII • JOE MORRIS: KEEPIN' IT CLEAN

have collaborated on numerous occasions, and the sounds they create together are beautiful and compelling—*Big Top* is an under-recognized record which should not have passed below the radar the way it did. Still, the soundmix is unfortunate. When Morris solos on a track, he's barely brought up from the subservient position he's placed in throughout the rest of the number.

The other preconception of the guitarist is a more rock-centric one, which arose after the fusion era of the late 1960s and early 1970s, due mostly to the cross-pollinating influence of John McLaughlin's work with the Mahavishnu Orchestra, the jazz-rock-Latin fusion of Carlos Santana's albums from the early 1970s, and the unremitting, almost heavy metal harshness of Miles Davis' mid-1970s albums like *Agharta, Pangaea* and *Dark Magus,* along with the aforementioned Sharrock, Bailey and Ulmer. All these figures combined, along with the players who followed behind them in the 1980s and 1990s, to create an atmosphere in the avant-garde which was far more conducive to screaming fretwork and noise than it was to small-group swing, and complex melodic structure. This is, to some degree, the audience which has arrived at free jazz through Sonic Youth guitarist Thurston Moore's advocacy of the form, and consequently their expectations of avant-garde jazz are met more by David Ware and Charles Gayle than by a soft-spoken, swinging, staccato guitar player working in a totally unadorned, distortion-free manner.

Morris understands the position he's in all too well. He chooses not to engage either camp directly, but rather to offer a third path. Through his own highly individual and uncompromising style, he challenges both sides to meet him where he's working. "I think jazz at its best is ritualistic," he told me. "That doesn't mean it's always a dark ritual. I've read enough about ethnomusicology to know the way an ethnomusicologist refers to these things, and that's that music serves functional rituals. It serves different functions for social ritual. A lot of times, people want their music to be really intense, to fully engage them, because when they're really engaged, they have a second where they can contemplate their existence. A split-second. Maybe a day. It wakes 'em up. Reading a great story does that. It makes you think about your own creative impulses for a minute. That's why I do this. I do this because this is the thing that makes me feel that way, and that's how I want to live. So I've always understood that about kids into punk. Of course, I'm the same age as the original punk groups, and I already had something I thought was much more extreme than that, so I was like 'I don't need that.' But I understood that what they were doing was trying to have an uncompromising musical experience. They didn't want it to be big and popular. They wanted to go to a little club, with a little group of aficionados, and just revel in the whole experience. They didn't want it to be a corporate entity. And that's what I'm saying about me. I don't wanna be the standard-bearer for commercial guitar stuff in the world. And when somebody says that new music guitar improvisation, Fred Frith or somebody like that is gonna do that, I walk away. Good. Have it. Take it. Be a millionaire. Because to me, that's exactly what—the reason I articulate everything is so that no one can go 'Yeah, man, it was really burning.' They go 'What was that?' They stop. They ask. It forces them to follow the pattern, and to become involved in details, rather than just taking the visceral and try to pass it along to everybody. That's already done. And other people will do that. That's a different function. It serves a different function. I'm not gonna criticize that kind of stuff, I never do. It's just that aesthetically, it's not what I'm about. I'm not competing with that. But I can understand why people are into really extreme subcultures of metal. [And] I understand that a lot of people like David Ware because he has a lot of power in what he does. And I don't really get the benefit of most of those fans, because I don't have a lot of power in what I do. But what I try to tell people is, if you want power, I play an electric guitar. I can go buy more power than any saxophone player on the planet for 1000 dollars. What I'm trying to do is the anti-power. I don't want power. I don't want that kind of energy. I want subtlety. I want melody, I want energy, I want swing, I want dynamics. The stuff I hear in Charlie Parker, the stuff I hear in [Eric] Dolphy, the stuff I hear in Thelonious Monk, Jimmy Lyons, Cecil Taylor, Fred Hopkins, Steve McCall, Anthony Braxton, those people. And David Ware [whose music, though it may be loud, is also extraordinarily complex and challenging]. That's what I want. Because that stuff is complex. The results you can get, the effect you can get off of that, is complex. Other things are simple. They're direct. They hit you right in the face. That's great. That's what they're trying to do. Congratulations. They do that. But I'm trying to—I think that exploring subtlety, quietly listening to things...I don't have pretense about it. I don't want people to meditate when they're listening to me or anything. I want people to come in, sit down, take their coat off, here's some normal people doing something that's pretty rarefied, and leave with a different experience. That's enough. It's like if they walked down the street and they looked at a tree. 'Man, it's a tree! It's amazing. It's growing up out of the ground...what the hell is that there for?' It's a very similar thing. If they go down the street and they see a big car wreck and they go 'Wow! That's incredible!' or they see a bolt of lighting, that's a different experience. It's more intense. It's too easy to do that with the guitar. It's too easy, for me, to do that. I know to do it consistently, with commitment, is a different aesthetic, so I would never put it down. But in this genre, to play like that is a cheap shot."

Morris' pursuit of beauty, and a certain spiritual quietude in his music, has led in a natural progression to his latest CD, the duo project *Soul Search*. An outgrowth of "Renascent," an improvised duet from the Quartet's *A Cloud Of Black Birds* release, *Soul Search* was recorded quickly and simply in Maneri's basement studio. Maneri, playing electric violin, provides much of the structure on the album's ten cuts, while Morris stutters out ideas, and dances around him. Though each piece is clearly separate from the others, there is an exploratory tone which unifies the disc. Because there are no rhythm instruments to shove or coax the two players in any direction, they proceed at a relatively slow pace, finding their way gradually upward and outward. *Soul Search* is a meandering conversation definitely worth eavesdropping on. It provides a glimpse of yet another side of Joe Morris, closely related to the music made by the Quartet but, in its own way, very different. The clearest indication of the depth of Morris' genius is how many facets emerge from what seems, on its face, like an extremely limited tonal vocabulary. While studiously avoiding pretentiousness or triviality, he has found a path to an incredibly detailed and multifaceted soundworld, one which provides him with seemingly limitless avenues for exploration.

• Daniel Carter

IX • DANIEL CARTER: THIS IS A TEST

New York's subway stations aren't the most hospitable environ ment for musical expression. Despite the vast array of musicians down there—saxophonists competing with violinists, acoustic guitar strummers, the occasional full electric rock band and even traditional Chinese musicians playing ancient instruments—amid the squawking of track announcements, the crash and roar of trains arriving and departing, and the head-down, eyes-front, gruff demeanor necessary to fend off repeated requests for alms from the City's least fortunate, who's got time or attention to spare for music?

The members of Test are convinced that Manhattan's harried commuters *do* have the time. In fact, they're convinced that the people of New York *need* their subterranean music. They are quite certain, individually and as a quartet, that what they offer is something the City, and the Earth, needs. For more than five years the quartet has been bashing out their brand of fully improvised free jazz on the platforms of New York's subway stations, week in and week out, with only occasional breaks to go on tour, or for the Vision or Fire In The Valley festivals. Or, as happened recently, to open a show for rock performers like Sonic Youth and Mike Watt.

Test, if such a profoundly collective ensemble can be labeled one man's idea, was the inspiration of its drummer, Tom Bruno. Bruno was performing solo, and doing occasional duos with other musicians, in the subways as part of the City's Music Under New York program. Musicians who participate in the program are assigned locations by the MUNY administrators, and are provided with subway tokens and occasional help finding other bookings. "I was in the program," Bruno told me, "and Daniel Carter was doing solo stuff. I saw him in the office, and thought I wanted to work with him. So after a trip I took to Berlin, I contacted him and we formed a trio with a bassist, Dan O'Brien." This group played together for a short time, but O'Brien soon departed. Enter new bassist Matt Heyner, and saxophonist Sabir Mateen. The lineup hasn't changed since.

When I first heard about Test, I was convinced I knew what it would sound like. A quartet featuring two saxophonists, a bassist and a drummer, performing on subway platforms. They had to sound like a duel between Albert Ayler and Pharoah Sanders, with a rhythm section whomping away behind them at full throttle and top volume. I couldn't have been more wrong. When I heard Test's self-titled CD on Aum Fidelity late in 1999, I couldn't believe this was the group I'd been hearing about. Test's music is shockingly introspective and exploratory, and reveals almost nothing about the circumstances of its creation and incubation. Or maybe, in some roundabout, oppositional way, it does. Bruno believes that working in the subway has very much informed the quartet's sound. When playing amidst the chaos of a train platform, "you have to be influenced by the commotion, and surmount the negativity of everything around," he told me. "By playing in the street, you become stronger. It's good for you, as a working situation." Bruno's attitude transcends any and all limitations. The minimal kit he works with underground (a 16" floor tom, a snare drum, a hi-hat and a cymbal) is, to him, an inspiration rather than a restraining force. "With a kit that size, you have to use your imagination, and stretch a bit," he says.

Test is as interesting to watch as to hear. Their sound may be about collective effort and communication between the members of the band, but their stances and postures don't reflect that at all. Bruno works his kit for all its worth; even when he's using brushes, it still sounds like he's using sticks. Bassist Matt Heyner, the youngest member of the group by at least 20 years, stares into space, plucking and occasionally bowing the strings in a trance-like state. It's clear from the angle of his head that he's paying close attention to everybody else. (Bruno says the group has been a tremendous learning experience for Heyner, who formerly played in the No Neck Blues Band. "He came in and took time to find his place," says Bruno, "and his solos are beautifully strong now.")

The two saxophonists, Sabir Mateen and Daniel Carter, face straight ahead when they play. Carter has a wide range of R&B honker stage moves; he tilts himself forward, leaning towards the floor like he's playing "Tequila" or a King Curtis composition, occasionally leaning back in particularly ecstatic moments. Mateen works in a similar manner. The one thing the two hornmen don't do, though, is look at each other while they're playing—at least not much. Each is totally lost in his own musical moment, never so much as throwing a glance at Bruno or Heyner, let alone the other saxophonist. For an observer used to the close, face-to-face football-huddle-like interplay of the David S. Ware quartet, or to the deep stares between Matthew Shipp and William Parker while they play, it's slightly disconcerting to see Test work in such a disconnected manner.

Part of this can be linked to the fact that Sabir Mateen, at least, has a strong individual identity outside the confines of the quartet. He has a trio album, *Divine Mad Love* (Eremite), and has worked for over twenty years as a sideman in groups like the Pan African People's Arkestra in the 1970s, the Raphe Malik Quartet, and the One World Ensemble (which also features Carter), among many others. Mateen and Tom Bruno have released a live duo CD, *Getting Away With Murder* (also Eremite), which was recorded in Grand Central Station; behind the music, it is possible to hear Bruno thanking commuters who tip as they pass by, and track announcements for trains arriving and departing, oblivious to the music. Another interesting Mateen release is his recent duo CD with drummer Sunny Murray, *We Are Not At The Opera* (again on Eremite). This concert, recorded at the Unitarian Meetinghouse in

Amherst, Massachusetts in 1998, is credited not as a duo but to Murray with Mateen, and that's the way it sounds. Mateen begins the album blowing soft spirals of notes on a flute, as Murray slowly ascends from delicate cymbal washes and rumbles of kick-drum to what will become, over the course of the album, an awe-inspiring and breathtaking drum solo. Mateen, even when he begins playing alto and tenor saxophones later in the performance, can often do little but keep pace with the drummer's titanic earthquakes of sound. Murray shows clearly on this album that he has lost little of his power, and none of his sense of rhythm and dexterity, since he first appeared on legendary albums like Cecil Taylor's *Nefertiti, The Beautiful One Has Come* and Albert Ayler's *Spiritual Unity.* Indeed, *We Are Not At The Opera* is but one in a recent trilogy of duo efforts by Murray. The others are *Illuminators* (Audible Hiss), featuring Charles Gayle, and *Dawn Of A New Vibration* (Fractal), with Arthur Doyle. On both of these releases, the horn players (Gayle plays piano for the first half of *Illuminators*) find themselves in the same position as Mateen, holding their own but certainly never stealing the spotlight from the massive, roiling storm that is the drumming of Sunny Murray.

The album *Getting Away With Murder* is slightly more delicate than the Murray duo, but it's just as vital and gripping a performance. Consisting of a single 45-minute piece, Mateen plays alto sax the entire time. Bruno plays his usual minimalist kit, using only brushes. The two musicians seem to be working together sometimes, and to be playing completely separate songs at other times. It's an interesting record, punctuated as it is by occasional murmurs of 'thank you' as Bruno acknowledges a tip. These vocal interjections can sometimes be quite funny, coming in the middle of particularly loud, hurricane-strength passages from Mateen. One wonders what the commuter must have been thinking as he dropped change, or perhaps a dollar bill, into the box.

Much of the aggression found in Mateen's duo discs is downplayed in his work with Test. This is, of course, due to his having to share the spotlight with Daniel Carter, a saxophonist who has his own highly individualistic ideas about expression. Carter, a tall, balding man, is fascinating to talk with, or—more accurately—listen to. When he gets going, it's hard to slow him down. His mind seems to move in a dozen directions at once. In conversation, he'll often begin discoursing on a subject and within five minutes, he'll be three tangents away from where he began. He winds his way back...eventually. In the meantime, the listener has learned about five or six different subjects, much more than they'd have picked up if Carter had simply answered the original question. This omnivorous, generous and casual intellectualism is also the perfect metaphor for his playing style. Carter, like Mateen, switches back and forth between multiple instruments. During the course of a single piece by Test, or his other main group Other Dimensions In Music, he will play tenor sax, alto sax, clarinet, flute, trumpet, or any combination of these.

Surprisingly, as he's primarily known as a saxophonist, Carter's first instrument was the clarinet. "I went for a saxophone at first," he says, "and we just about had it purchased, and then it seemed like somehow somebody made a U-turn, either my mother or my father found out something or the guy that was selling it to us alerted us to the fact that it was a C-melody saxophone instead of an E-flat or a B-flat." Carter couldn't find a use for a C-melody saxophone in his school band, so he picked up the clarinet instead. "The C-melody just became outmoded or something," he says. "Not that it didn't play, but they weren't writing music for it or anything." The C-melody, which is constructed like an alto but plays in a higher range, is indeed one of the weird, forgotten offshoots of the saxophone tree. Not many people play it, other than Peter Brötzmann (who plays virtually every reed instrument, including the Japanese tarogato), and Jim Sauter of the upstate New York power-jazz-improv trio Borbetomagus.

Carter first began playing around New York in 1970 or 1971, which was when he met William Parker; although he says his memory's fuzzy on the exact date. The two were playing in a big band led by alto saxophonist Jemeel Moondoc. Later, Moondoc formed Ensemble Muntu, which featured Roy Campbell on trumpet, Parker on bass, and Rashid Bakr on drums. As Carter says, "Other Dimensions In Music is Muntu without Jemeel, and Muntu is Other Dimensions without me." Moondoc has never been a widely-known performer. He still records and performs, though, and Carter still admires Moondoc greatly. "I always felt," he says, "and still do, that Jemeel is one of the most unique voices, as a player and as a human being, and I think that it's maybe not the total fault of the people out here on the planet today, particularly in the US, and in other parts of the world I think it applies too, people are being flattened and steamrolled into some flatter, less rooted [form] in the sense of ethnicity and cultural language, gesture, movement, uniqueness. [Authenticity] seems to be less desirable, unless it's a museum, or somebody from acting school is learning to play the part. We really don't want the real thing. We want to have enough of it so that we can clone it, so we can duplicate it and then the clone is under our control and won't cause problems. But the real thing is too much. [People want] just enough that it won't mess up the advertisement."

Carter worked here and there in the early to mid-1970s, but over time his highly individualistic style, the total freedom with which he approached any situation, became somewhat of a professional liability. "I was getting to a point where I was maybe a little frustrated," he says now, "because I'm always trying to find a positive, diplomatic way to say this, but in certain ways—I won't say that I was this outrageous monster, I wouldn't even say that now, in terms of how I play or whatever. But from some other people's point of view, they just naturally wouldn't call me, or they would call me less, because if I wasn't an outrageous monster, I was an aspiring anarchist. Not in the sense of disorder, everything is crazy in the street, violence, but in the sense of wanting to be myself as much as possible, and...sometimes you discover you're radically different in your procedure. You have no real desire to be radically different in your procedure, and to clash with the procedures of others or the methodologies of others, but I got to the point where I didn't want to be told what to do." Fortunately, in 1981 Other Dimensions In Music came together, and provided the perfect forum for Carter's wide-ranging instrumental journeys. Carter's in-the-moment approach could be seen as the perfect demonstration of the theory which supposedly underpins free jazz—that it's possible to snatch melody and beauty from the air without thinking about it for hours, or even minutes, beforehand. This faith in impulse and inspiration is the root of all jazz, but Test and Other Dimensions In Music are prime, perfect examples of what happens when theory, in the hands of master musicians, becomes practice.

Even though he has found what could easily be considered ideal circumstances in these two groups, both of which play fully improvised music all the time (neither Test nor Other Dimensions approach a recording session or a live performance with any idea what they're going to play, or hear from their bandmates), Carter recognizes that this isn't the path everyone chooses. "Sometimes you cover such ground," he says, "and you get into the area you want to with the people that you can really get with, and you forget that all these people you're working with, they work like that, but maybe still the vast majority of people don't work like that. But because these are the people you work with day in and day out, month in and month out, year in and year out, you're so fortunate to do that, that you're not even thinking about the way other people work. This is your regular life. And then you come up against something, and you're reminded, this is your regular life, but this ain't other folks' regular life. This ain't other musicians' regular life. Still, largely, today, in music, somebody gets ideas, and they compose music. They get some words, or they get a chord, or a melody, or a rhythm, and they start pinning it down, or at least remembering it, and communicating it to other musicians. But we [Test and Other Dimensions In Music] don't work like that. Except that, however, at the same time you want to put all those words [composition, improvisation] in brackets. Like in the case of Other Dimensions In Music, if you think of some people who in one way or another, close, distant or indirect, have been acquainted with or know each other in some cases as long as 28 or 29 years and in all cases no less than 22 or 23 years—the community of musicians is small enough that when people know each other like that, even if they're not playing with each other a lot, it immediately comes to mind what that vibration is." In other words, even though the group may be improvising at full speed, in a spirit of total musical freedom, each of the four knows the others' personalities, musical and otherwise, well enough to have some idea where the music's likely to head. As though anticipating a question as to why a group might continue for as long as Other Dimensions has, in light of the risk that the players might gradually come to absolute predictability [this being the reason the improvisatory jazz-rock-noise quartet Last Exit gave for disbanding after just over three years—they didn't want it to become predictable], Carter continues, "And then not to say that it's not constantly, in some cases brutally, challenging you. I mean, God knows, if a person is awake, they're challenging themselves."

One of the most important ways in which Test challenges listener expectations is the relative quiet of their music. In some ways, it would be easier for them to simply blare at full strength and attempt to outdo the trains and track announcements and cell-phone conversations and all the other ambient noise that fills New York's subway stations. But instead, Test pieces often spiral inwards rather than rocketing outwards, and the music is all the more rewarding for it. "First Peace That Ever Was, Is, To Be," the first cut on their self-titled Ecstatic Peace album, from 1999, is a perfect example. (Test released three CDs, and one LP, in just over 18 months. The Ecstatic Peace album was in fact recorded in 1996, though it took three years to see daylight—when it did, it was accompanied to store shelves by another self-titled CD, on Aum Fidelity. A few months later, Eremite released *Live/Test*, a disc recorded on the group's November 1998 US tour. Eremite's vinyl sub-label, Nowjazz/

IX • DANIEL CARTER: THIS IS A TEST

Ramwong, has released *Ahead,* recorded on the same tour but containing different material.) "First Peace..." is a slow, carefully building 26-minute exploration of sound which never becomes obstreperous or even extroverted. It seems to demonstrate the four musicians delicately tiptoeing around one another in the studio, offering brief flurries of notes in turn, but the group as a whole never settling on a consensus or a specific direction. It reminds the listener of a play by Samuel Beckett, wherein one character says "I can't go on" only to be told by another "You can't stay here." It's a restless piece, the members of the quartet scuttling about as though trying to find out the limits of the space, not because they're going to do any one thing or head in any one direction—they just want to know what they're working with. The other two tracks on the disc, "Dis-Astor Place" and "A Journey into the Love, Light and Power of the Creator—Part 1," are significantly louder, the latter piece (which incorporates shouted interjections at its ecstatic peak) being, as its title might indicate, very much in the emotive, pyrotechnic vein of later Coltrane pieces like "The Father And The Son And The Holy Ghost," from *Meditations.*

The (also self-titled) Aum Fidelity disc, which was recorded in label head Steven Joerg's apartment one afternoon, is also a somewhat scattered set of music. The primary characteristic is, again, introspection, with only the final track, "what RU going 2 due?!," being in any way aggressive. "That day," Carter recalls, "I was not as centered as I really would like to be. In a way I could say I hardly ever am, but that day I was particularly unsettled. Maybe I was hoping that I would be able to adjust for that. At some point I don't even try to keep myself together, I say well, it seems to be about disintegration or being blown apart, so if I can put that in the microphone—but it goes back to what my mother used to say, 'Contain yourself. You have to contain yourself.' I'd interpret that as stifle yourself, but if you think about it another way, like in the barrel of a gun...in some way that energy is contained, but it's being channeled, and a bullet itself contains that which can be ignited.

But that day I didn't feel at my best in those regards. But I'm sure everybody in the band had a different perception and a different goal from each other, and of course that's what really makes counterpoint. We're really not necessarily trying to do the same thing, but it is all-important...to keep the group together. It's like an atom, where you have all these differently-charged particles opposite to each other, but still holding together."

This sort of scientific analogy leaps to Carter's lips quite often when discussing the music he makes, and music in general. He is fascinated by science, particularly astronomy. The day we spoke, he had spent the previous evening watching a documentary on the origins of the universe, and it was consuming his consciousness as we conversed. "When you see it," he said, referring to a computer-animated illustration of the movements of galaxies, "and the way it moves, it's not a huge stretch to make a relationship between how this stuff moves and the way sometimes the music moves. There's so much information in it, and yet it can be what some people might call chaotic, but there's a positive sense of chaos and a negative sense, like there's a positive sense of anarchism and a negative sense. Or you have a sense of being bewildered by so much stuff that's not ordered, or structured, or you have a sense of, like, Schoenberg or Webern or Cage or Elliott Carter or Charles Ives, where even though you've got something that you can't handle all at once, you know it's together." Later in our conversation, Carter used the example of the Big Bang to tie together a theory about the many facets of the so-called "avant-garde," and how the contributions of dozens, if not hundreds, of musicians are often limited or misperceived by neophytes who know relatively little about the music, save a litany of names.

"One of the interesting things about all this music that's developed since the late 1950s," he said, "like Mingus, and when Ornette Coleman came to town in 1959 or so, the development of the New York underground, is that there's such a range of people. There's far more players than seem to have gotten to the point of being highly recognizable or remembered. Now, you can just imagine—and this gets into the Big Bang thing again, all these stars, all these planets, all these galaxies—each one of them. Imagine that you're one of trillions of things that maybe look a little like you, but you're unique, there's nobody else like you, nothing else like you. So can you imagine all the different relations, affinities, disaffinities and everything in between each one of those people and traditional jazz. Here these people have been blown out the other side, through the looking glass into this whole new music. But where were they blown out from? Probably from being listeners of Max Roach, Mingus, Ellington, and so at certain points, even if it can be rebellious, or disruptive, or nostalgic, or even just recognition or acknowledgement, like say Archie Shepp. It seemed like from early on he was celebrating the older guys, consciously, even with his first emergence." Carter sees this as natural, since in order to rebel against something, particularly in music or any art form, it's necessary to understand what's being rebelled against. "If you're fighting with somebody," he says, "you're in a heightened relationship with that someone." This is a perspective that's apparently shared throughout the New York community of players, and it's made evident in albums like David Ware's *Surrendered,* Matthew Shipp's *Pastoral Composure,* and the William Parker Trio CD *Painter's Spring,* on which Carter plays.

Painter's Spring is a fairly simple album; the three players (Carter on saxophones and flute; Parker on bass; Hamid Drake on drums) work their way through a series of Parker compositions, Duke Ellington's "Come Sunday," and the spiritual "There Is A Balm In Gilead." Carter's solos on the disc never head for the outer limits, but remain firmly grounded in the blues tradition which underpins all of jazz. In many ways, *Painter's Spring* is reminiscent of a quieter, more restrained jazz of the 1950s or early 1960s—the kind of record that might have come out on Prestige or Savoy. "I think that [simplicity] was part of the vision of that," Carter says about the record. "I think that maybe speaks to dimensions, and other dimensions of music. There are other dimensions of people. Other dimensions of genres. And these genres can help each other tremendously. You have people who for the most part are listening to this genre or that genre, and then they get a chance to hear something from another genre, and it doesn't discourage them, it encourages them to check it out." Carter seems to believe that records like *Painter's Spring* not only expand the listeners' conception of what free jazz players can and should play, it benefits the players too, drawing them out of the (somewhat paradoxically) constrictive realm of formless, go-for-broke improvisation. "It's possible," he says, "that if people had a chance to develop what's in them in a way that was less constrained to even be avant-garde in the first place...I mean, a lot of these things probably would not have even come into being if conditions in life were much better. It creates these certain pressures where stuff has to erupt, because it couldn't be healthy, normal circulation, and exchange of ideas." And beyond the realm of pure aesthetics, there lies the much larger, and more forceful (some might say destructive) realm of market forces. "Take rock 'n' roll for example," Carter says. "Rock probably would have permeated, intermingled much more with classical, jazz, different aspects of jazz, country music, which is where it came from, different musics from around the planet, but you've got these market categories, and you've got people who want to produce you or have you perform somewhere, and they have to know what kind of stuff you're doing. And the musicians get a little concerned, and they say hey, we gotta make sure this is clearly this, and even if they like something else they say oh, I can't do that over here. Sometimes it's because of individuality, because somebody is an individual, but how do you tell? Is it the individual, or did some force, political or economic, make it that way?" This is what makes Test, and Daniel Carter, important. By taking the music directly to the people, addressing harried commuters whether they're ready for it or not, and by offering pure, totally unrestrained expression at all times, Carter and his bandmates open a window to an expansive vision—not only of music, but of life, fully and creatively lived, in real time, all the time.

• Little Huey Creative Music Orchestra

X • PUTTING ON A SHOW FOR THE PEOPLE

Becoming a master musician is difficult enough, but that's only Step One. Finding performance spaces that will welcome your particular sound and musical concept is a whole other matter. Over the decades, there have doubtless been dozens—if not hundreds— of players who have given up in disgust and gone back to their day-jobs, simply because there was no place to play the music they wanted to play.

The jazz clubs of New York have long been notoriously hostile to free jazz. In the music's earliest years, there were small, dingy East Village bars like the Five Spot (where Ornette Coleman debuted), and later Slug's Saloon. Players like Albert Ayler and Pharaoh Sanders, frozen out of the big-name clubs like the Village Vanguard, gathered, performed and commiserated in these back rooms, plotting a sonic revolution that never quite came. The tourist-trap clubs—the Vanguard, Sweet Basil, Iridium, the Blue Note and Birdland—are just as closed to free music now as they were then. I've seen Cecil Taylor at the Village Vanguard, and Pharaoh Sanders at Iridium, but Cecil Taylor is Cecil Taylor—a living legend and guaranteed to sell the place out—and Pharaoh Sanders has mellowed considerably in the past thirty years. Musicians wishing to play free music have a few basic choices. There are two clubs hospitable to avant-garde jazz in New York right now. One more so than the other. A few other, basically unknown, venues (the Cooler, the Internet Café) book the occasional one-off show, but if you are a free jazz musician and you want an audience, you're going to appear at either the Knitting Factory or, more likely, Tonic.

The Knitting Factory, in the years since it moved from its Houston Street digs to its current lavish, multi-leveled location (74 Leonard Street), has done its best to paint itself as the Temple of Avant-Garde Rock and Jazz in New York. Whether this is entirely true or not is immaterial; substantial advertising dollars have been expended to create that perception. Yet, through his annual jazz festival (which, due to lack of funding, did not take place in 2001), club owner Michael Dorf has been assiduously moving towards the mainstream. The festival, which began years ago as the What Is Jazz? Festival, eventually became known as the Knitting Factory Jazz Festival. In the past few years it has been substantially expanded, and underwritten by major corporations like Texaco and Bell Atlantic. As this happened, the festival's scope widened considerably. In 2000, it encompassed everything from a lavish all-night tribute to Ornette Coleman, to concerts by Lou Reed, Sonic Youth and Stereolab. Astonishing events have been made possible through this influx of corporate cash, including the first duo performance by Cecil Taylor and Max Roach since 1979 (for which the David S. Ware quartet served as the opening band).

The Knitting Factory itself, though, has always been more comfortable with the Downtown "new music" aesthetic than with hardcore free jazz, and therefore performances by the Ware group, or Charles Gayle, are comparative rarities, punctuating a schedule clogged with indie-rock bands, art-rock holdovers and postmodernist Jewish music. This was even more prevalent before Dorf and John Zorn had somewhat of a falling out; for a while in the mid-1990s, barely a week went by that some Zorn-related event was not on one of the Knitting Factory's multiple stages. With a record label, a substantial Web presence, the annual festival (to which, whatever the corporate sponsorship may be, the Knitting Factory brand-name is prominently affixed), and a location in Los Angeles, the Knitting Factory is establishing itself as a franchised clearinghouse for a very specific slice of the "avant-garde."

While all this goes on, Tonic (107 Norfolk Street) has been quietly emerging as the most interesting new avant-garde music venue in New York. A small, dark room with perhaps fifty chairs and standing room for fifty more people, the club has become the center for all the truly interesting music seemingly no longer welcome at the Knitting Factory. Tonic has built its reputation on a somewhat novel booking style, contracting with a musician to book all the shows for a given period, featuring artists of the booker's choice. The club's first two months were booked by John Zorn, and included the biggest names on the Downtown music scene. With virtually no fanfare, this tiny space has become the hottest destination south of Houston Street. While Tonic books rock bands and "new music" acts as well, the club has become a home away from home for the New York free jazz scene. Other Dimensions In Music have played there, as have Charles Gayle, Matthew Shipp, Mat Maneri, Joe Morris, Roy Campbell's Pyramid Trio, and Peter Brötzmann's Die Like A Dog Quartet, among many others. In recent months, Tonic has been packed to the walls for shows by Cecil Taylor—first, a duo performance with iconoclastic British guitarist Derek Bailey, and later a series of duo performances with drummer Tony Oxley. The intimacy of the small venue makes it an ideal place to see and hear live jazz. Without the steep door-prices of the tourist-trap clubs uptown, or the herd-'em-in, herd-'em-out-again atmosphere of rock clubs (lingering from one set to the next is, if not encouraged, acceptable), Tonic has the potential to become one of the places, like the Five Spot or Slug's, memorialized in jazz lore.

Interestingly enough, in 2001 the club scene has morphed once again, thanks to the event which brings the New York free jazz community together each year. That event is the Vision Festival, which in its sixth year has broken with its history of unorthodox spaces (the Learning Annex, the Orensanz Arts Center, St. Nicholas Of Myra Church, the New Age Cabaret) and moved into the Knitting Factory, with larger-capacity shows taking place at Orensanz. The Vision Festival has become symbolic of a dramatic resurgence in the vitality of free jazz, and its audience. Moving the whole thing "indoors," so to speak, into a year-round performance space, gives it a solidity which removes the impression that the festival is something which congeals out of the air for two weeks each year, and then vanishes again as though it was never there, bolstering the organizers' credibility when it's time to get mainstream media coverage. This isn't some hippie party, it's a major jazz initiative—particularly in a year when there is virtually no other place for fans of vital, engaging improvised music to turn. And, more importantly, it brings the "downtown" and free jazz scenes closer together than they've been in years. Despite Michael Dorf's total lack of involvement—he's hosting the Vision Festival at his venue, but he has no role in determining who gets to play—the symbolism of it is clear, and positive, both for the festival and the Knitting Factory.

The Vision Festival is a unique event in New York's ferociously competitive music scene. There are no souvenir T-shirts for sale. There are no corporate sponsors. There are no viewpoints heard but those of the artists, channeled through the philosophy and heart and—yes—vision of one woman: Patricia Nicholson. Nicholson, a dancer, and the wife of William Parker, is the driving force behind the Vision Festival, and has been since its inception in 1996. She also organizes the "Mercurial Visions" shows at the Mercury Lounge which, for the past two years, have provided a one-night, mid-February preview of the festival to come. Ten or so of the major performers on the scene play improvised sets, in combinations determined the same evening, with dance accompaniment and art installations livening up the Mercury Lounge's usually dingy decor.

Nicholson and Parker have always been independent operators. It was a necessity, given their desire to work together not only behind the scenes, but onstage as well. "We self-produced from the beginning," she says, "that's what you did. There weren't very many—especially what we did—there were almost no venues that produced us, that did dance and music. Back in the 1970s, that was not accepted very much in New York. I don't think this was true in other places, but in New York, the dance community wasn't interested in avant-garde jazz, and the music community hated dance. I mean, they would get angry sometimes. And so there was very little—this isn't necessarily as true for the musicians as for the audience. Although the musicians, then, were also less open to it. Because it was like, for them, I think, there were more people then who were not into it than there are now. It was seen as...I'm talking about a lot of young musicians—they were young at the time, they're not young anymore—they were all excited about what they were doing in the music. And they weren't being accepted, and there was a sort of slightly...defensive stance. Which was understandable. And so they— not all, but some of them—were like, What do you want? Because the dance tends to take center stage, because it's more visual. And they felt like it might upstage them, or encroach on their turf. It was a matter of turf."

Nicholson and other artists have presented dance as a vital part of the free jazz scene at the Vision Festival each year. In 1996, five dancers—Nicholson among them, but also Rod Rogers, Maria Mitchell, Simone Forti, and Elaine Shipman—performed to various levels of musical accompaniment. Rogers danced to music by pianist/ multi-instrumentalist Cooper-Moore; Mitchell danced to solo bass by Peter Kowald; Forti performed alongside saxophonist Daniel Carter; Shipman interpreted a duo by Matthew Shipp and alto saxophonist Rob Brown; and Nicholson danced to music by a trio of saxophonist Assif Tsahar, Parker on bass, and Denis Charles on drums. Similar collaborations have taken place at each year's Festival, always to warm response from the audience.

The Vision Festival is hardly the couple's first effort at organizing performances. Nicholson and Parker have always strived to create awareness of their chosen art forms, and to expose the work of others as well. One particularly prominent event the two worked on was the Sound Unity Festival in the mid-1980s. "That was an event that was initiated by Peter Kowald, with a grant that he was given to do it, and he did it with William and I helped, the two times it occurred," Nicholson recalls. The first festival took place in 1984, with a follow-up in 1986. Among the performers at those festivals were players who would continue to appear at other New York events, including the Vision Festivals: drummers Rashied Ali and Milford Graves, David Ware, Charles Gayle, Peter Brötzmann, the late trumpeter Don Cherry, and John Zorn. A documentary film of the first festival, *Rising Tones Converge,* is available on video, though its distribution leaves something to be desired.

Zorn's, and by extension the "Downtown" crowd's, participation in free jazz events has always been something to be greeted with ambivalence, not to say suspicion, by both sides. Nicholson, though, has done her best to close the sometimes acrimonious gap between the "Downtown" crowd and the free jazz players. "[Zorn's] involvement in that festival was because Peter Kowald bridges back and forth," Nicholson explains. "You don't want to be defined by the way other people define you and the way that people break these divisions up. So these divisions, and who is responsible for them, I feel like in Sound Unity and the Vision Festival, we don't think that those divisions are good. I mean, I think you should look at a musician as someone who has a voice. They have their own voice, and they have their own music that comes through them and what they are really interested in doing and all that."

Unfortunately, following the Sound Unity Festival, the free jazz scene drifted back to the obscurity it had suffered since the late 1970s, while the "Downtown" scene flourished, relatively speaking. It was nearly ten years before Nicholson was able to make anything substantial happen. When she did make her move, though, it began a process which has yet to slow down. In the early 1990s, she says, "the scene just felt like it was dying out. The only time people got together, where there was any sense of community, was at a funeral. So it literally felt like the scene was dying out. It was really depressing. You'd just hear about one funeral, then another funeral, and that was it, and then there wouldn't be anything else. So I started the Improvisers' Collective really to build community. And people got together who hadn't seen each other for years. I just called up a whole lot of people, and we did it." The Collective began presenting shows at Context, a studio on Avenue A which continues to host occasional events to this day. "The first year, we produced two concerts a week, and the first half of the night would be a presented program, and the second half of the night would be an open improv that would be led by whoever was leading the presented part. So they would stay for the second group, and it could be any way they felt like putting it together, or not...you could do whatever. But you needed someone to be responsible, so that would be whoever's gig it was that night. So we did that twice a week, I think from the end of January 1994 till—in June we had the Improvisers' Collective Festival, and everyone was presented. We had dancers, a few poets, musicians and Jeff Schlanger, the visual artist. The only visual artist who was a member at that time. Then we took off the summer and started again in maybe November. The second year, I got a little help from Assif Tsahar. He helped me with the publicity. I did almost everything the first year, and then the second year he started writing press releases. Again, we finished the second year out with a festival. By the end of the second year I was really tired of this. We had stopped doing the open improvs because there wasn't that much interest in it. So we started doing one night a week, and there were two groups that night."

Things might have slowed down at that point, as the Improvisers' Collective shows had worn Nicholson and Parker out pretty thoroughly, but a surprising overture kept their interest up. At this point, William and Patricia had become close with the young saxophonist Assif Tsahar and his then-wife, drummer Susie Ibarra (who replaced Whit Dickey in the David S. Ware Quartet). Tsahar suggested to Parker and Nicholson that a new collective be organized, which was not members-only (as the Improvisers' Collective had been). "We were just talking," Nicholson says of this fateful discussion. "We weren't exactly ready to do anything. But on the other hand, I'm a doer, and Assif had a lot of energy." Additional energy, and support, arrived then from an unexpected source. "There was this guy," Nicholson says, "who had been coming to concerts, who publishes what's called the Open Pamphlet Series, a fairly political press. They put out stuff by Noam Chomsky and people like that." The publisher, Greg Ruggiero, "came up to me and said, could you get the musicians to do a benefit for us, cause they needed to raise some money. And I said, Well Greg, I don't know if we can really do a benefit. Because the musicians are in such bad shape. Things may not be great now, but they were much worse then. Things have really changed. I mean, not as much as they need to, but they were really bad then. So I said, 'It can't be a real benefit, because the musicians need benefits.' That's how I felt. So I said, 'Why don't we just do something together, and then we'll give you a percentage of the door.' That was the idea. And then, he had access to this space...we didn't have to pay for the space, so maybe we could make it work. And it turned into the festival. The first Vision Festival, in 1996. The first Vision Festival ran from June 5 to June 9, at the Learning Alliance on Lafayette Street. Over 40 musical groups, poets and dancers performed during those five days. According to the festival program,

> The Vision for The 21st Century Arts Festival [the original name, now shortened] presents art on the terms that uphold and expand the concepts of each musician, dancer, painter and poet—those who have died and laid down the tracks and those who are still creating. A masterpiece is an ongoing project that lasts a lifetime. Art must be presented, it must be seen and heard. It is for the enrichment of all those who attend and those who do not. It is about lights shining and not being buried. It is ultimately about the greatest art, that is, living.

Nicholson says "The thing about the first Vision Festival was, it was an absolutely inspired event. It was just the right thing at the right time and I felt it. I really put us out on a limb," she says now, laughing. "Because I guaranteed everyone money, and I had...I had one grant of $2500, and I was running a five-day festival. People were working for a low amount of money. We paid everyone almost the same thing. It didn't matter who you were, sort of. The only time we didn't guarantee was, we had a Saturday afternoon thing which we didn't guarantee money for. It was because we wanted to include everyone, so we did that. William kept saying he thought it was crazy. We made jokes, and said we'll get David [Ware, a somewhat legendary fan of fast cars—riding shotgun with him gets the adrenalin flowing better than most roller coasters] to be the getaway man."

The response to the first festival was incredible, when one considers the virtual media blackout on free jazz at the time. "I think the budget wound up being $25,000," Nicholson says. "And we made it. We made it off the door." As time has gone on, of course, expenses have increased—most notably because the musicians have begun to receive better payment for their performances. "The whole point of it was not to get artists to work for low fees. The point of it was to build up this art form. And part of that means demanding a living wage. So you don't want to talk people down too much on their price."

The question of who appears at the Vision Festival has become a thorny one over the years. Though there is a clear nucleus of the New York scene—all the artists covered in this book, and a few others besides—there are many more performers whose profile is smaller, but whose music deserves a public hearing. Nicholson does not choose the acts for the festival herself; a panel of musicians on the board of her organization, Arts For Art, does that. And as the Festival has become one of the more fascinating cultural events of the New York year, the clamor for spots has become close to overwhelming. "This is becoming more and more true every year," Nicholson says, "but this year [2001] it's ridiculous. What I tell everyone is, we don't take requests for gigs. The musicians select who they want to present. But if you want to let me know, I'll make sure that they consider your name. It becomes such pressure. I have at this point—the festival's only nine days [in 2001]. And approximately four groups per day, that's 36 groups. I've probably had about 100 requests."

In the weeks following my conversation with Patricia Nicholson, the scope of the 2001 Vision Festival expanded quite a bit. There were a total of thirteen days of performances. The festival opened on May 24 at the Knitting Factory, and ran there until June 2. There was a five-day break, and the whole event decamped and resumed on June 6 at the Orensanz Arts Center, where it remained until closing night on June 8. Performers included the figureheads of the New York scene—David Ware, Matthew Shipp, William Parker's new quartet—but also included shows by Peter Brötzmann and Chicago tenor saxophonist Fred Anderson, among many others. The festival operated under a larger theme, "Vision Against Violence." This was not something which Nicholson attempted to throw over all the performers and performances, like a blanket. After all, instrumental music is often fascinating precisely because of the latitude for interpretation which it grants the listener. Overt musical politicking can all too quickly become tedious. Rather, the theme was present more in the visual arts on display (sculpture, painting and dance); musicians were left free to address it, or not, as they chose.

It goes without saying, given Nicholson's history with the Sound Unity Festivals, that not all the performances at the Festival are by traditional free jazz musicians. This can be a mixed blessing. On the one hand, genre barricades were broken down somewhat when, as in 1997, John Zorn performed a duet with drummer Susie Ibarra. That same year, the Festival went even further a field, sonically, offering performances by organ groove-trio Medeski, Martin & Wood, and a trio centered around Sonic Youth guitarist Thurston Moore. Zorn returned in 1999 (this time duetting with percussion master Milford Graves), as did Moore. Sometimes these events work well, fitting into the context of the festival as a whole, and sometimes they don't. "The crossover booking doesn't always work," Nicholson says. "We've outreached to Zorn's crowd. That does not work well.

But when we did Zorn with Milford Graves, that did well. But Zorn's people don't necessarily pull well. That whole group doesn't necessarily draw at the Vision Festival. We'll always do crossover booking, but on the concept that...you don't want to lock yourself in. Creatively, it's bad; in terms of community, it's bad; politically, it's bad. Who you outreach to varies. But you have to come up with things you think are going to be a success. You have to have good audiences every night, because it makes it feel good. Not just because we need the money, even though we're very door-dependent."

One of the strangest events, both in terms of actual sound and of impact on the Festival, took place in 2000, when Matthew Shipp and DJ Spooky performed as an improvising duo. The very concept of these seemingly musically antithetical players—Shipp the pure free jazz pianist, and Spooky the poster-boy for the "Illbient" school of turntable-and-sampler poetry—appearing together onstage, interacting in real time, caused a substantial attendance spike for that night; it was the most attended night of 2000's festival. The performance itself was not particularly earth-shattering; each player stayed thoroughly ensconced within his own style. Shipp offered cluster-bombs of notes and returned often to a motif lifted from Dave Brubeck's "Take Five;" Spooky hurled a few different beats in the pianist's path to see if they'd make an impression, and when they didn't he moved on to other tricks without looking back. The most interesting moments came when Spooky sampled Shipp's playing on a laptop and played snippets of it back at him, rhythmically, allowing the pianist to improvise on the notes he'd played only a moment or two before. But overall, however conceptually interesting it may have been, the results were less than spectacular. The performance was extremely well-received, of course—the free jazz fans applauded the effort, while the postmodernist hipsters there to check Spooky's latest move offered reflexive approbation. A noble experiment, it didn't fail utterly; nor was it a rousing success. Except in terms of door receipts. Still, one thing about the performance annoyed Nicholson and the other festival promoters, and that was the media reaction to it. "I wasn't upset that there was all that audience," Nicholson says, "I was happy there was all that audience. I was upset that one of the few pictures in the *New York Times* was of DJ Spooky."

The myopic press coverage of the Festival is a persistent irritant to Nicholson. "Zorn became almost our poster boy," she says. "His picture was the one that was most often asked for in relationship to the Vision Festival. That's annoying. It's inappropriate and annoying." Newspaper coverage of the Festival is often written from a perspective of ignorance, or misperceptions. Worse, a few critics review the shows, every year, from a puzzling angle of ill-disguised hostility. Ben Ratliff, the *New York Times* reviewer, depicts the Festival as something to be ridiculed—its organizers to be gently patted on the head for their effort (however misguided)—rather than as a genuine cultural event to be appreciated on its merits. The *Village Voice,* whose jazz critic, Gary Giddins, is often perceptive and appreciative of free jazz, also does little to publicize or review the festival. Giddins doesn't even attend as a listener. The greatest appreciation for Nicholson's efforts has come from magazines, particularly *Jazziz.* "Larry Blumenfeld's [*Jazziz's* former editor] been incredibly supportive," Nicholson says. Indeed, *Jazziz* has been one of the few magazines to run consistent, and favorable, articles on the New York players. In 1998, the magazine printed a lengthy, and considered, review of a Vision Festival performance by a one-time quartet consisting of saxophonists Charles Gayle and Kidd Jordan, bassist William Parker and drummer Milford Graves, who had never played together in that combination.

The Vision Festival, at its best, is more than just a collection of musical performances; the audiences and the musicians become one mass of people, interacting before, during and after the specific sets. It is always possible to walk in and see musicians gathered in small groups, talking amongst themselves or with other fans. Roy Campbell, in particular, is a consistently-accessible figure, smiling widely as he holds court in a room adjacent to the performance space, talking to whomever comes by and sits down at his table. The thing which first drew me into the free jazz scene, even more than the power of the music, was the sheer friendliness of the atmosphere. The Vision Festival has none of the attitude seen and heard at uptown jazz clubs, where customers not dressed to impress are seated in the back or by the kitchen door and the musicians stalk to the stage and off again with barely a word to anyone.

This positivity, and openness, is something Patricia Nicholson is understandably proud of. To her, it's part of a larger continuum of social interaction mixed with politics, which has formed her worldview for decades. "From the very beginning, I was very happy when Greg Ruggiero approached me, because it gave [the Festival] a political context, a social awareness context. Not political, socially aware. 'Political' has so many other connotations, 'socially aware' is more what I'm really concerned about. We need to be socially aware, we need to believe in things, because I think that one of the ways we're defeated is by thinking that there's no hope. People have become so used to the commonness of evil. The daily-ness of it. We take it for granted and we think that there's nothing you can do about it. We don't even notice it anymore. That's the way it is, I have no power, there's nothing you can do. But there are things you can do. Evil exists, and goodness exists, but if you don't believe that you can do good, then evil becomes stronger. So people need to believe that they can do good, and that their goodness makes a difference. And the more they do, the better they'll feel, and the better the world will be. I mean, I'm not gonna make every bad thing go away, but don't be so ready to be so-called pragmatic. This is the way it has to be, and compromise. Be real, not pragmatic. What are we really doing here? Let's not doubletalk anymore. Be simple about—I mean, there is such a thing as right and wrong. There are a lot of good people. When you're doing good, you're not alone. One of the biggest weapons they use against you is to make you feel powerless. But of course there are things you can do. Every time you behave righteously, with a real caring for the human beings whose lives you touch immediately, and the greater world around you. One of the reasons we called it the Vision Festival was because, although the word vision has been used in such a way that it's losing its meaning, I believe in visions. And if you take your visions seriously, your visions become reality. I believe in dreamers, and making those dreams real. But if you want to make them real, you have to let people have them. You have to encourage a little dreaminess. Because people have times where all they're doing is sitting around and dreaming dreams, and when it's the right time they stand up and make them happen. You have to let people have their process. The whole process is good. But you do want them to come true. You do want them to be not just something in your head." The Vision Festival has become a dream which is shared by hundreds of people each year. It has become the one gleaming thing the entire free jazz community—musicians, poets, writers, painters, sculptors, and listeners—looks forward to each May. Everyone involved goes into it knowing that their lives will be filled with music, art, and conversation which will last them the rest of the year, and beyond.

• Matt Heyner (bass) I Daniel Carter (sax)

XI • LIES JAZZ CRITICS TOLD ME

When I began this book I had no intention of discussing the Ken Burns-directed PBS documentary *Jazz*. I'd already heard the advance murmurs: that it might as well have been directed by Wynton Marsalis; that it just *stopped* at 1960; that it was bullshit, inaccurate, effectively a work of fiction. Unfortunately, between then and the time of this writing, *Jazz* has become an unavoidable subject. It's reached every corner of the jazz world—it's been met with praise, debate, and loud groans of disbelief and disappointment. One writer I know told me that if Ken Burns' version of jazz is what jazz truly is, then the term refers only to a form that is long dead, and the avant-garde must find a new term, and leave the very word "jazz" to the conservatives who assembled the film.

What can actually be said of substance about *Jazz?* Does it have any message to communicate to those interested in free jazz, or even listeners already familiar with jazz? Yes, and no, on all counts. Assuming, as we will here, that the series is an abortion and a travesty, there are two obvious defenses available to those seeking to take Burns' side, and the side of his advisors—Wynton Marsalis, Stanley Crouch, Albert Murray and Gary Giddins, among others. Both have been repeated ad nauseam in all sorts of media since the film made its premiere in January 2001. The one heard most often tells us *Jazz* is the only large-scale effort to address the genre, to date, and naturally there will be mistakes made and names omitted. In other words, we the viewers should be thankful the filmmakers gave us anything at all—even if what we got turned out to be a 19-hour biography of Louis Armstrong, with a few tangential comments about musicians who would never have played a note had not the sainted Satch descended from heaven to bless us with his golden horn. (Gary Giddins is such a brilliant writer, with such a keen understanding of nearly every facet of jazz, that to see him bleating, in utter seriousness, about how Armstrong's trumpet playing was "enough to make the angels weep" was nearly enough to make *me* projectile-vomit.)

The second big defense being mustered up for the series is that it will, thanks to its multi-million-dollar ad campaign, bring a whole new audience to jazz. People who've never heard of Charlie Parker will go out and buy his records after they see the documentary. In other words, it's not aimed at jazz listeners—it's aimed at an untapped market segment. Ken Burns has, in fact, been quoted as saying he doesn't care about the jazz audience. What longtime listeners think about the distortion of the music's history is not his concern—he's got a story to tell, and he's going to tell it. Fundamental errors in the structure of Burns' myth, though, leave even a minimally knowledgeable viewer with questions. Why does the film claim to stop in the early 1970s, for example, but then pick up again to detail Wynton's riding in like the cavalry to save jazz from all that awful fusion and avant-garde clatter? Why is the last segment (a discussion of new performers who are supposedly bringing young, hip listeners to jazz) devoted to Cassandra Wilson, whose audience is made up of boomers and geezers—in other words, the typical tourist-trap jazz-club crowd—rather than Matthew Shipp's and David Ware's co-optation of punk and alternative-rock audiences? We're not told, and Burns would prefer we didn't ask. The subtext of this defense (which takes the form of a dismissal of any criticism, however justified) is, of course, the virulent anti-intellectualism that characterizes 90 percent of discourse on any subject in contemporary America, particularly matters of culture. If those who actually understand and love jazz complain about *Jazz*'s hypocrisy or its distortions of history, we're elitist snobs, trying to keep "the people" from joining our secret club.

Jazz critics are like legal scholars or yeshiva students—they like to return to the text, they like to be able to cite precedent. This leads them inexorably towards the whirlpool known as the Great Man theory. The Great Man theory is a prism through which to view history, insisting that history is always motivated by the actions of great men—singular, iconic figures who stand against the tide and become magnets for Destiny. This is the stylistic template followed by *Jazz*. One towering figure became symbolic of each era of the music's history: And lo, Louis Armstrong begat Duke Ellington, who begat Charlie Parker, who begat Miles Davis, who begat John Coltrane. And then there was twenty years of wandering in the desert, until there came among the people Wynton Marsalis. And he did play his horn, and it was good.

Unfortunately, this theory doesn't jibe with the real-world version of jazz history, post-1967. In June of that year, when John Coltrane died, jazz effectively lost its last Great Man. Miles Davis was still alive, but a year later he broke up his last acoustic group, and by 1975 he vanished entirely, in a haze of freebase smoke and electric guitars, having—in many critics' eyes—turned his back on jazz in favor of some sort of hellish funk-rock attempt at cashing in. (How anyone could listen to records like *Big Fun, Get Up With It* or *Agharta* and think of them as pop-chart moves is beyond me, but that's the argument made, in total seriousness, by conservative critics.) In the 1970s, jazz splintered, and multiple allegiances were declared. Some followed Miles into electric, rock-oriented fusion. Others, like the Art Ensemble of Chicago, investigated African rhythms and poetic introspection. Cecil Taylor continued to be Cecil Taylor— iconoclastic, brilliant, and utterly consumed with exploring his own musical concept, whether anyone was paying attention or not.

Obviously, there's no way for the Great Man theory to take hold in such a Balkanized artistic landscape. There's no way a historian in search of easy answers—or at least a matinee-idol to symbolize jazz in the 1970s—can be expected to work with this kind of fragmented, divergent music world. So Burns chooses to simply turn his back, and worse yet, papers over the hole in his story with the idea that not enough time has passed for "history" to weigh in on the great figures of today. This, of course, doesn't account for the film's treatment of Marsalis, or even (less egregiously) the quickie montage of young, up-and-coming stars tacked onto the end like a pitch to investors. "Jazz—a still-vital brand name looking to move proactively into the new century!"

Of course the documentary isn't a total wash. Far from it. Burns claims that he was ignorant of jazz when he began the project. If that's true, it's admirable that he devoted himself to the subject as deeply as he clearly did. It would have been easy to create something like *VH-1's Top 100 Albums Of Jazz*. Watching this series, I learned a lot about a few performers whose work had previously been unknown to me; for example, I knew nothing of Art Tatum's music before watching *Jazz*, but now, he's on my list of players to investigate. For years, I've been mostly ignorant—and largely disdainful—of big-band swing. After watching *Jazz*, I'm ready to go pick up some Count Basie discs. I'm hoping the same thing happened across the country. More people should buy albums by Clifford Brown, Bud Powell, and Sonny Rollins (each of whom is the subject of discussion during the series). But they should also buy records by Cecil Taylor and the Art Ensemble Of Chicago, and with *Jazz* as their guide, they won't. Taylor is the only musician to be openly criticized in the entire film. He's quoted as saying that he prepares for his performances, and the audience should be prepared as well. This isn't an unusually egotistical statement—if someone wants to appreciate a Jackson Pollock painting beyond the visceral rush of staring at the swirls and splatters of color, it's best to understand what Pollock was aiming for when he painted it. But Branford Marsalis is trotted out to call Taylor's request for intelligent, probing audience members "self-indulgent bullshit." Similar, though more subtle, is the dismissal of the Art Ensemble Of Chicago.

Throughout the film, Burns continually filters jazz through the prism of American race relations. He also fails to acknowledge the contributions of anyone, or anything, born outside the continental US to the music, thus totally ignoring Dizzy Gillespie's popularization of Latin jazz, French Gypsy Django Reinhardt's virtual invention of modern jazz guitar, and numerous other things. Given the primacy of racial issues throughout the film, not to mention its rabid America-first attitude, can it be anything but an implied smear that the Art Ensemble's audience is described as primarily "white college students in France"?

Well, carping from me, or anybody else who actually knows what Ken Burns was talking about (or, more accurately, not talking about), for all those weeks on PBS isn't going to have the slightest impact. *Jazz* is a hit. Early reports are that the *Jazz* boxed set is selling ferociously well. The individual compilation CDs of artists spotlighted in the series are also heading off the shelves at a good clip. But CDs that don't have Ken Burns' name on them, that exist purely as music, without the stamp of PBS respectability, are by and large languishing in the racks, collecting dust the way they always have. It makes me wonder what it would take to actually get people to buy jazz without a brand-name imprimatur on it. Mainstream jazz magazines surely aren't going to help much.

Though the quality of criticism varies—that is to say, it doesn't all suck, all the time—the aim of jazz magazines is to inform existing jazz listeners, not to convert new people to jazz. It can't be. A specialty magazine, whatever its focus, is by its very nature aimed at people who are already enthusiasts. Nobody expects *Model Railroader* magazine to offer articles on building military dioramas. By the same token, *Down Beat* shouldn't be bothering itself attempting to entice folks to jazz who've previously been interested in punk rock. The only way to get jazz the new audience it needs (as discussed in Chapter One) is to head in the reverse direction—covering the music in mainstream, broad-focused music magazines that have not previously covered jazz. This is what's been happening for the last few years. Fresh, unheard voices are piping up from previously unnoticed corners. And considering some of the writers who've been making jazz their beat for the past few decades, that's a damn good thing.

It's the easiest thing in the world to complain about bad press. Every artist is convinced the critics don't understand them, and the litany of dismissals is always the same—"critics only do it for the promos"; "critics are just frustrated musicians"; "I never read reviews." Most of the time, though, the artists are right. Music criticism has about the lowest entrance threshold of any form of writing. You don't need to know *something*, you just have to know *somebody*, to become a record reviewer for some tiny, zero-circulation rag somewhere. And if you're persistent enough, you work your way slowly up the journalistic food chain to incrementally more respectable publications.

Admittedly, most young writers do start out with some passion for the work. They're filled with the burning desire to tell everybody in the world about *their favorite band.* They'd better be, too—the life of a music critic is a tough one, economically speaking. Magazines don't pay much, and it's a constant scramble to find work. Unless a writer can grab a staff position at one of the few outlets with any kind of financial stability, he's going to be frantically scraping up whatever freelance work he can. This is true of both rock and jazz magazines. The biggest pitfall to being a rock critic is that many magazines don't pay at all, or pay so slowly that it's barely worthwhile to write for them. There's also the pitfall of having to treat rock bands with the respect commonly afforded kings, rather than what they deserve, which is more often than not a two-by-four in the chops.

Every jazz magazine I'm aware of at least pays its writers (there's no zine culture in jazz like there is in underground rock), but there are so few of them that the range of opportunities for wannabe jazz critics is sharply limited. The best solution, for a career-minded jazz critic, is to make himself a friendly and cooperative servant of the interests that top the jazz food chain. The process common to art criticism, whereby an established critic champions an up-and-coming painter or sculptor, is inverted in the world of music journalism. The up-and-coming writer must find record labels and artists' managers who are willing to throw him the scraps (liner-note commissions, for example) which will make the writer's name while increasing or cementing the public profile of the artist. Thus does deference to power take the place of nuanced listening in the critical process.

There's no percentage in being known as the chronicler of free jazz, though. This is one reason why free jazz takes the abuse it does (only gangsta rap and Satanic black metal, in the rock/pop arena, come in for the critical pasting free jazz gets). None of the artists a writer might choose to hitch his wagon to are likely to provide the dividends that can be earned as the hagiographer of a Wynton Marsalis, or even a Brad Mehldau. Therefore, many jazz writers see criticism of free jazz as a chore, or an apprenticeship program through which they must pass before being permitted to write about "real" jazz.

A perfect example of this phenomenon is the career of *New York Times* critic Ben Ratliff. Ratliff appeared in New York as a fresh-faced kid, looking for something he could grab onto and call his own, journalistically speaking. He found it in the music of the free jazz scene. Matthew Shipp and David Ware, and to some extent William Parker, took Ratliff into their confidence and, early in his career, offered him what assistance they could; he wrote the liner notes to Ware's *Flight Of I,* Joe Morris' *Elsewhere,* and a few other albums. Sensing an opportunity to make his name, Ratliff's notes were a suitable blend of effusion and deference. Even then, though, there was a snide undertone in his work. He praised Morris ably enough, saying, for example, "But to view abstraction in music not as a chasm but as pure possibility, as the occasion to record a particular vision—controlled of course, by the style, grace and circular intuition of the players—well, *now* we're getting elsewhere." But this was countered, even in a liner-note assignment, by snippy asides like "Even among the best free improvisers, a style once used in the service of keeping clichés at bay can be hardened into orthodoxy." It seemed as if, even as early as 1996, Ratliff was gearing up to turn his back on this music, once it had served his needs. (Both quotes are from the liner notes to *Elsewhere*.)

Over time, Ratliff made a name for himself, and eventually, he moved into the positions he currently occupies, on the staff of the *Times* and as a regular contributor to *Rolling Stone, Jazziz,* and other magazines. As his fortunes have risen, though, his careerism has become more obvious. Now that it no longer serves him to respect the music which gave him his earliest commissions, he strives to give off the aura of worldliness and success so crucial to his development as a genuine New York critical institution. Openly disdainful of free jazz, he still reviews the Vision Festival each year, and other related events and albums, but the articles are filled with scorn for his former compatriots—calling the music "cultural rebellion for pre- and post-hippies," and the like. It's the Crouch trick all over again; after all, Stanley came into the scene riding David Murray's coattails and only turned into free jazz's most public enemy once he'd become a critical institution. It's a shame nobody saw it coming with Ratliff—the second time around, you'd think the signs would have been more apparent.

At least Ratliff displays occasional flashes of talent. If nothing else, he can turn the odd phrase. Unlike Howard Mandel, author of *Future Jazz* (Oxford University Press, 1999), who may be the worst writer covering jazz today. If he isn't, I have no interest in finding out who is; having read the book, the idea that there could be a writer with less understanding of his subject matter than Mandel is too painful to contemplate.

Future Jazz, cobbled together from the few moments of lucidity in Mandel's work from the 1980s through the mid-1990s, illustrates the greatest gulf between title and contents of any book it has ever been my displeasure to read. Mandel's blinkered concept (it can hardly be called a "vision") of jazz's future is most easily illustrated by his decision to make a three-part interview with Wynton Marsalis the framing device of his tome. For surely, if a book is called *Future Jazz,* what could be more appropriate than to spend nearly twenty pages energetically fellating the man who has made it his life's work to turn jazz into a tuxedoed repertory company, mindlessly parroting the musical methods and styles of 40, or even 70-plus, years ago?

Aside from Wynton Marsalis, Mandel's vision of jazz's future also finds room for George Benson, Michael Brecker, and Cassandra Wilson. Notably absent are any of the artists under discussion in this book—apparently, when Mandel ventures out of the high-priced tourist-trap jazz clubs in search of slumming kicks, he checks out the "Hasidic New Wave" musicians playing at the Knitting Factory. Of all the artists in this book, the only two whose names appear in *Future Jazz* at all are Matthew Shipp and Charles Gayle. Neither are discussed; instead, their names appear on lists, to show that Mandel has heard of them (Shipp is not cited as a leader, which he had been for seven years before *Future Jazz* hit shelves, or even for his work with David Ware—who does not appear at all in the book—but as someone "who has worked in Roscoe Mitchell's band"), even if he doesn't actually consider their music as "futuristic" as that of, say, David Sanborn.

All the musicians who don't merit discussion in *Future Jazz* have the following, seemingly unforgivable qualities in common:

> No one of these musicians is yet crossing over to a general public, writing songs that are on so many lips that they get bought up for commercial jingles. None of them is making a fortune as a performer or recording artist—and it's fairly unusual for any of them to be courted by the sorts of not-for-profit American institutions that would project them to the arts-consuming elite. Their creations—and the work of legions of their peers—might be thought anachronistic, rooted in the big cultural bang of the late '60s, so avant-garde as to have no chance of being claimed by mainstream artists or audiences, so peculiar that they get put down by conservatives as less of an advanced front than a lost patrol.

In Mandel's world, to have failed to find one's way to the bank is to have failed artistically. Never mind that jazz musicians haven't been making serious coin by selling pieces for commercial use since the days of Lee Morgan's "The Sidewinder," in 1964. Still, this attitude is perhaps understandable, given the man's own industrious prostitution of his (questionable) literary talents. An ideal example is provided by the Art Ensemble of Chicago's album *Dreaming Of The Masters Vol. 2: Thelonious Sphere Monk* (DIW, 1992). On p.40 of *Future Jazz,* the record is dismissed with the following: *"At least one track from the AEC's effort with Taylor deserves attention:* in 'Caseworks' Jarman and Mitchell play flutes, and Bowie essays a characteristic phrase, first to introduce, then to overlay, and finally to mistily waft away the pianist's prototypical motifs." [Italics mine.] Contrast this not-exactly-positive summary, then, with the following:

> The Art Ensemble has throughout its career explored the balance of individual contributions, interactions and blend. 'Intro to Fifteen Part 3A' is a splendid event resulting from Malachi Favors Maghostut's intuitive structural sense, Famoudou Don Moye's range of touch and dynamics, Lester Bowie's overarching tone, Roscoe Mitchell's flowing and probing soprano sax, Joseph Jarman's precise and spare saxophone remarks—offset by Cecil Taylor as both call *and* response, foundation *and* embellishment.

And this, too:

> Whatever *you* hear in Monk's indestructible compositions, the Art Ensemble's detailed realizations and Cecil Taylor's passionate imprecations *are* there. As a listener, you create the conditions of the moment, without which this music doesn't exist. That is not to imply the concrete fact of this recording is negligible. On the contrary. *Dreaming Of The Masters Vol. 2* invites the dream to recur. [Italics in original.]

Substantially more effusive than the one-sentence dismissal afforded the album come book-contract time: the words above are from Mandel's own liner notes to the AEC/Taylor disc.

Gary Giddins, who's been the *Village Voice's* jazz critic for what seems like a century, is practically Mandel's polar opposite. Concise and coherent, his columns and books are some of the best writing on the music, period. He seems to possess a genuine love for jazz in almost all its facets. Sometimes the catholicism of his tastes lends itself too easily to squareness (he's working on a multi-volume biography of Bing Crosby), but his appreciation for the avant-garde, and his understanding of its place in the tradition, is unmatched. Giddins' book *Visions Of Jazz: The First Century* (Oxford University Press, 1998) is a marvelous work, virtually the ideal starting point for people looking to get inside the music and understand where to begin listening. He provides histories and appreciations of many of the major performers, from the earliest "hot" jazz groups to the free players of past and present, all with equal affection. No one is singled out for butchery, the way Cecil Taylor is in the PBS documentary *Jazz* (as described above). Naturally, the totemic figures—Duke Ellington, Charlie Parker, Louis Armstrong—get more space than some might feel they deserve. After all, what more can really be said about Armstrong, Duke or Bird that's going to surprise anyone at this point?

Overall, the book is the best survey effort anybody's likely to publish anytime soon. A slew of avant-garde artists are profiled in its nearly 700 pages, including Cecil Taylor, Ornette Coleman, Muhal Richard Abrams, Roscoe Mitchell, Henry Threadgill, Charles Gayle, David S. Ware, Matthew Shipp, Hannibal Peterson, Julius Hemphill, Don Pullen, Gary Bartz, David Murray and Don Byron. Giddins' tone, though, is the most impressive thing. The mere fact that he printed the following paragraph, in a book aimed at the widest possible jazz audience, is all the evidence anyone should need of his love of the music, and his value to the scene:

> Conservative rhetoreticians who patrol the arts for agitators often revert to literalism as a kind of mockery. They hold a generic phrase to the light, find it wanting, and conclude, Q.E.D., that any art so designated must be wanting, too. 'Free

jazz' gets them blathering about discipline; 'new music' about longevity; and 'avant-garde' about military divisions. The most common and yet inexplicable insult of all is the idea that extreme forms come easy. No one believes that Gaddis and Rothko had it easier than Bellow and Wyeth, but in jazz the suspicion that Albert Ayler was somehow cheating, while no longer as rampant as it once was, is far from dead. Having passed the fortieth anniversary of Cecil Taylor's Jazz Advance, though, it ought to be clear that, metaphorically accurate or not, avant-gardists don't ride ahead of the mainstream legion; the two help keep each other honest.

Giddins is, unfortunately, an exception among high-profile jazz critics. (Francis Davis, writing in the *Atlantic Monthly*, has excellent taste, but publishes far too infrequently to be any kind of serious voice for the music.) Most hew far too closely to the Ratliff/Mandel (and, by extension, Burns) model. This is why, since the beginning of the 1990s, some of the most exciting and vital jazz criticism in America has appeared in the pages of rock magazines. Reviews of avant-garde and free jazz records, along with profiles of the major figures in the music, have been appearing regularly in magazines like *Alternative Press, Option* (RIP), *Magnet,* and countless zines, for years now. *Magnet,* a magazine whose cover is always devoted to some college-rock sensation or another, features a column in each issue by Bill Meyer, detailing recent free jazz releases. Players like Matthew Shipp and David Ware have been the subjects of lavish profiles in rock magazines, often garnering a significantly better reception than the reception they receive in jazz journals.

But mere column inches don't help if the coverage is shallow and boneheaded. So it's even more interesting to note that rock-mag reviews of free jazz albums, in many cases, are more valuable to students of the music than the jazz mags' take on the same discs. For example, David Ware's *Surrendered* was reviewed in *Down Beat* alongside John Tchicai's latest release, *Infinitesimal Flash.* (The Ware/Tchicai review was one of only two split-artist reviews, out of fifteen full-length reviews in the May 2000 issue of the magazine.) When I was pitching reviews of the disc to rock-oriented websites and magazines, though, I had no trouble getting solo review space.

The approach taken to the music in rock magazines differs, as well. This should be obvious, but it bears mentioning. When free jazz records are reviewed in jazz outlets, the approach is so uniform it commonly reeks of a style-manual. This, again, was detailed in Chapter One. For example, James Hale's review of *Surrendered,* in *Down Beat,* begins with the following: "The biggest carp against the free jazz revival of the '90s was that those listeners old enough to appreciate the historical context thought they had heard it all before. 'Yeah, Charles Gayle can blow,' they'd say, 'but I saw Shepp and Trane together.'" Why is this dismissive tone not employed against those musicians who continue to mine the same chord changes mainstream jazz players have been working since the 1940s? How is that "a formidable knowledge of the ancestry that preceded him" (to quote a John McDonough review of a Benny Green disc, in the same issue) and the other a "revival," with that word clearly chosen to evoke images of Civil War reenactment groups or oldies cover bands? The disjunction is so obvious that it has become unworthy of comment in most quarters. It's simply the prevailing point of view, and it's the rare review that breaks with tradition that winds up receiving notice.

In rock magazines, by contrast, free jazz releases are weighed on the merits of the music, rather than against some imaginary standard of historical revisionism wherein bebop clichés somehow remain fresh and exploration of post-1960 ideas are historical throwbacks. Consequently, a rock listener reading about David S. Ware in *Alternative Press* is more likely to feel that the record merits investigation than a jazz listener stumbling across the review in *Down Beat.* (By the way, does it bear mentioning that there are exceptions to this trend in jazz journalism, exactly as there are exceptions to every other sweeping statement—that mainstream jazz magazines have, from time to time, printed quite excellent analyses of free jazz performers and their music? Perhaps it doesn't, but please consider these two sentences sufficient disclaimer.)

The one major jazz magazine to have devoted what I consider sufficiently respectful attention to free players is *Jazziz*. The magazine, while under the stewardship of recently departed editors Larry Blumenfeld and Dante Sawyer, quite often devoted cover space to avant-garde musicians. David Ware, Matthew Shipp, William Parker and the Art Ensemble Of Chicago all received major cover stories in the magazine between 1997 and 2000. Joe Morris and Mat Maneri were also recently profiled, side-by-side but in two separate articles by two different writers (Steve Dollar interviewed Morris, while Ed Hazell investigated Maneri). At the same time, *Jazziz*'s review section was, and remains, one of the only places where it is possible to read criticism of free jazz unburdened by the mock-historicist approach delineated above.

What all this says is that jazz journalism is as stuck in the past as the majority of the music is. An attitude of reverence for the totemic figures of the first half of the century, and a refusal to value and reward the kind of sweeping new efforts that could quite easily bring in the new listening audience the music so sorely needs, is dooming jazz as surely as the mortality rate among its greatest surviving players. The promotional campaign undertaken in support of David Ware's second (and final) Columbia album, *Surrendered*, is a case in point. Rather than buy dozens of ads in small-circulation indie-rock magazines, which would have added up to thousands of additional sales from rock fans already familiar with Ware's work through reviews of his independent releases throughout the 1990s, the label chose to buy one or two ads in mainstream jazz magazines, and leave it at that. The audience that buys *Jazz Times* or *Down Beat* is unlikely to buy a David Ware album. There's a portion of *Jazziz*'s readership that will (and did) buy the record, but even in *Jazziz*'s case, it's doubtful that any jazz listeners took a chance on the album if they weren't already Ware fans. This dismal miscalculation on the part of Columbia's jazz division is bitterly ironic when one considers that *Surrendered* is a much more palatable album than its better-promoted predecessor, *Go See The World*, and could have, with the right kind of promotion, been a substantial success (by jazz standards). Just a slightly better college-radio and alternative-rock-magazine promo campaign could easily have translated into additional sales. (And with Wynton Marsalis' dozen-disc vanity project *Swingin' Into The 21st*—a series of discs released roughly one a month for the atter half of 1999 and the first half of 2000—tanking dismally in stores, Columbia really could have used Ware's help.)

Sadly, it doesn't seem that any lesson can penetrate the status quo of major-label jazz procedure. If they did things any differently, they wouldn't be jazz labels. At this point, the only strategy that makes any sense for free jazz artists is to sign with independent labels, and advertise in the rock underground. The audience exists. The music exists. Tiny, barely-breaking-even rock magazines, and the basement indie labels profiled in the next chapter, are bringing the two together.

• Mat Maneri

XII • GETTING IT ON TAPE

I f you want real, compelling, music, pick up an independent release. For virtually the entire history of recorded music, independent labels have been releasing the most edgy, off-center, creative records. (The only possible exception would be the class of '77 punk rock acts—Blondie, Talking Heads, the Ramones et al., who were all signed to majors.) Witness the emergence of Elvis Presley, Johnny Cash, Jerry Lee Lewis, and Carl Perkins (to say nothing of lesser-known rockabilly titans like Sonny Burgess, Billy Lee Riley, and Charlie Feathers) on tiny Memphis indie Sun Records. The list of great rock artists harvested by majors from indies would be miles long.

In jazz, the same theory holds. Savoy and Dial Records, home to the greatest music Charlie Parker ever recorded, were both independents. Blue Note began as an indie label, before being bought by EMI/Capitol as a reissue project. Impulse! Records, which released John Coltrane's most introspective and brilliant work, was an independent label, as were Prestige, Riverside, and Verve, each responsible for releasing astonishing music by Thelonious Monk, Sonny Rollins, and virtually every major jazz figure of the postwar era. In the post-bop years, during which the avant-garde emerged, jazz owed even more to independent labels for its continued vitality. Labels like ESP-Disk, India Navigation, hat Art (a label created specifically to release records by saxophonist Joe McPhee) and hundreds of other, infinitesimally small indies released albums by artists no major label would touch. This without even mentioning artist-owned labels like Sun Ra's El Saturn, or Charles Mingus' short-lived Debut. The independent label is one of jazz's longest-lived, and proudest, traditions.

From both the artist's and the consumer's perspective, indie releases are a great bet. The artist, though he may not get a huge advance for his work, will receive a higher royalty rate on the CDs he sells, and may wind up selling more records than he would have on a major. If a major picks up your album, and decides not to promote it, you can wind up going on tour only to find that your record's not in any stores in the towns you're playing. This has happened to rock acts from the Rollins Band to No Doubt. Independent artists are often tied into a network of like-minded folks across the country, so if the record's out, people know about it without having to look for ads in a glossy magazine. Tours are announced by e-mail and word-of-mouth, or on a website run by the label, rather than by extensive pre-show advertising. The consumer, when buying an independent release, is more often than not getting the artist's vision, virtually undiluted by outside input. Often, it's possible to stumble across a new voice and hear it develop over time.

Independent labels not only document individual artists, they often paint a portrait of an entire scene or subgenre. SST Records' work with southern California bands like Black Flag and the Minutemen—not to mention Hüsker Dü and the Meat Puppets—helped create the modern underground rock scene in America through their bands' relentless touring—booking shows into any venue that would have them, and bypassing the then-standardized rock pathways entirely. Warp Records, in the UK, has become synonymous with a particular style of abstract, intellectualized electronic dance music. Brooklyn's WordSound Recordings has spent nearly a half-dozen years documenting and expanding the zone where hip-hop meets dub. The most famous example of the modern era, of course, is likely Seattle's Sub Pop Records, which gave rise to the "grunge" rock movement. Even Def Jam Records started life as a dorm-room labor of love.

The New York free jazz scene has three primary labels which release the vast majority of records. Each has a specific focus, and is run by a single figure with a particular aesthetic, determining not only who is recorded, but in what manner and towards what purpose. All three have been in business roughly the same amount of time. The owners know one another, and coexist cooperatively. Because of their respective focuses, there's no real overlap; each one offers something different, and valuable, to the listener. Albums released on Aum Fidelity, Eremite and No More Records present three very different visions of the same music, and allow jazz fans to hear the music as a whole very differently than they otherwise might.

Aum Fidelity Records, based in Brooklyn, has the highest profile of the three labels. Started in 1996 by Steven Joerg, the label will have released fourteen CDs by the end of 2001, including albums by the David S. Ware Quartet, William Parker's groups (In Order To Survive and the Little Huey Creative Music Orchestra), Joe Morris, Test, the Whit Dickey Trio, and Other Dimensions In Music. Joerg occasionally hosts live performances at Aum Fidelity "Hi-Q." When Mat Maneri's quartet appeared there on a Saturday night in January 2001, pianist Craig Taborn wanted to use a Hammond B3 organ that was in Joerg's kitchen, so the show took place in the living room (the organ being too heavy to move upstairs to the normal playing space).

The label has become symbolic of the New York free jazz scene as a whole, not only because of the quality of their releases (something shared by all three labels) but because of the tireless energy with which Joerg promotes the label and the artists. Aum Fidelity advertises more heavily than Eremite or No More, and sends out many more promotional copies than either, securing reviews in numerous magazines—from underground publications to major national media outlets—in the process. Joerg has the admirable desire to build up appreciation for these artists' work during their lifetimes, rather than—as so often in jazz—decades after their deaths. Virtually every Aum Fidelity release has been reviewed in *Alternative Press* and/or *Magnet,* for example. However, the difference between Aum Fidelity and the other two front-running free jazz labels is greater than mere issues of art vs. commerce. Each label has a particular vision behind it, and Aum Fidelity's is one of creating classic albums, and a label profile to match.

Joerg got his start in the record business at the dawn of the 1990s, working as a promotion man for Hoboken, NJ indie Bar/None Records. The label was primarily songwriter-based and alt-rock focused, releasing records by They Might Be Giants and other college-radio friendly acts. He apprenticed there for two years, then moved to Homestead, the in-house label of major underground and alternative record distributor Dutch East India Trading, where he was appointed label manager. Homestead, in the late 1980s, was a major underground-rock force, releasing classic albums like Big Black's *Atomizer* and Sonic Youth's *Bad Moon Rising.* In the early 1990s, though, it had slowed down and scaled back, as its then-president, Gerard Cosloy, moved on to found New York uber-indie Matador Records (home of the Jon Spencer Blues Explosion, Pavement, Liz Phair and other widely-beloved acts of the "alternative" boom). Joerg, with a significantly slimmed roster of artists, began casting about for a way to make his mark on the label and the business, and that arrived in the form of Matthew Shipp.

Shipp's record *Zo,* a duo with William Parker on Texas indie Rise Records, was distributed by Dutch East India Trading. The pianist was a common sight in the offices, stopping by to check on CMJ airplay reports and sales figures. When he and Joerg met, they quickly became friends. "One day," Joerg recalled, "he brought in *Third Ear Recitation,* the Ware quartet record on DIW...because he sensed a receptivity in me to this music. And so...I brought it home and it properly blew my mind. He came back a couple of days later and was like, what'd you think? And I said well, I loved it! It's an incredible record! Thanks so much for giving it to me! And he was like, oh, cool...and that afternoon I got a fax from David, saying I heard you enjoyed the record, we're performing on Friday if you'd like to stop by. It hadn't actually gone through my mind that he was looking for an American deal, or that he was looking to be signed, because what I knew about his previous recordings—this was on DIW, the previous one was on DIW, *Flight Of I*...I was quite literally shocked that he was looking for a label. I went and saw the group at the old Knitting Factory, it was a small narrow space, it was packed...I was mesmerized." Joerg quickly began attempting to sign Ware to Homestead, but he got some early (and understandable) resistance. "I brought it to the owner of the company and the sales manager...and they were like, oooohhh...we're not a jazz label, Steve, we're not a jazz distributor, I don't know, I don't know. To which I said, don't be absurd. I viewed it as one of the greatest opportunities that the label had to have a significant impact on a whole other realm. I viewed it as a profound opportunity just to be able to work with [these artists], but I also saw that it could be successful." It was. "When I e-mail [Dutch East India Trading] now about buying those masters back, I get no reply," Joerg revealed. "Because it was successful."

The two Ware CDs, *Cryptology* and *Dao*, created a substantial stir in both the jazz and rock scenes. Jazz critics were shocked to see a major avant-garde saxophonist recording for a rock label, and indie-rock folks were astonished that Homestead would take a chance on jazz. The label, under Joerg, eventually released seven free jazz albums: Joe Morris' *Elsewhere*, the two Ware discs, William Parker's In Order To Survive album *Compassion Seizes Bed-Stuy*, two releases by drummer William Hooker, and *Cama De Terra*, a ferocious drumless-trio album by Brazilian saxophonist Ivo Perelman, Matt Shipp and William Parker.

Joerg's rock background, and album-oriented ear, explains a lot about Aum Fidelity's releases. Though the work is, naturally, the artists' vision, he takes a fairly active role in commissioning music and shaping it before it goes out the door. Joerg is a firm believer in the construction of albums, from the artwork to the sequencing of material, and not typically one to settle for documenting a performance when that performance can be punched up or excerpted and combined with other, equally powerful pieces of music. The only "one-take" disc in the Aum Fidelity catalog is Other Dimensions In Music's *Time Is Of The Essence; The Essence Is Beyond Time,* which documents a single live performance from December 1997. By contrast, each of the double-CD sets released by William Parker (*Sunrise In The Tone World* and *Mayor Of Punkville* by the Little Huey Creative Music Orchestra, and *The Peach Orchard* by In Order To Survive) are carefully culled from months of live performances. The material on *The Peach Orchard* is gathered from four sessions, recorded between February 1997 and March 1998. Similarly, *Mayor Of Punkville* was recorded at four separate Little Huey performances between July and November 1999. "I'm really into making albums," he explained to me. "They're documents of what a band sounded like at that point in time, but they're also conceptualized after the session into albums [because] I'm interested in dealing with the commercial marketplace and trying to appeal to a range of people, and make it more known to a range of people outside of the narrow bandwidth that is the fans of avant-garde jazz. Listening through to the pieces, choosing the best, most compelling takes, and then sequencing them into the arc of an album that is designed to be listened to at home—that's what you do. I do it in full collaboration with the artists, of course, but that's one of the creative outlets I have. I do the graphic design, and I also sequence the records, as far as putting them together to have a particular flow, to engage the head in a particular way, to tell a story in a particular way, to show strengths in a particular order."

The opposite approach is taken by Michael Ehlers, owner of Amherst, Massachusetts' Eremite Records. Eremite's catalog is almost exclusively composed of live tapes, many of them recorded at the annual Fire In The Valley Festival, which Ehlers curates. There's a reason for that. Ehlers firmly believes in the concept of documenting the music live, as it happens, and releasing entire performances on disc. "This is a concert music," he told me. "It's a communal music. Jazz has been a performing art for its entire history, and concerts are where this music really happens. So [Eremite's tilt towards live records] probably reflects a bias I have towards concert music." Though it might seem odd to base an avant-garde jazz label in Amherst, Massachusetts, so far from the typical major-city epicenters of musical activity, Ehlers claims to be only the latest in a line of free jazz proselytizers from the area. "There's a history of avant-garde jazz up here," he told me. "Marion Brown lived up here, and Archie Shepp was a tenured professor at the University of Massachusetts. During the 1970s and 1980s, in Amherst, U Mass and Hampshire College used to present jazz. There was an earlier free jazz label up here, too—Sweet Earth Records. They put out records by Marion Brown, and Sun Ra. They used to have PO Box 821; now Eremite has Box 812."

Eremite's records, unlike Aum Fidelity's, are minimally packaged; the vast majority come in monochrome sleeves, with black-and-white photos on the cover and simple liner notes. Artists' names, when the group doesn't have a specific name like, for example, Glenn Spearman's Trio Hurricane, are listed in alphabetical order, rather than the traditional listing of lead instruments first, followed by rhythm instruments. Everything about the label seems geared towards a simple appreciation of the music for itself, without much worry over packaging or image. (The word "eremite" is an Old English version of "hermit.") Eremite, in capturing live performances, has captured some truly astonishing material on its CDs. (Test has released three CDs and an LP thus far—studio recordings on Ecstatic Peace and Aum Fidelity, a live CD on Eremite, and a limited-edition live record—with different material—on Ehlers' sub-label, Ramwong. The live CD is by far the most powerful of their works I've heard.) One of the label's greatest services to the free jazz public, though, is not its work with established groups like Test, or Peter Brötzmann's Die Like A Dog Quartet, but its presentation of players whose names are not nearly as well known as they should be, such as Raphe Malik, Jemeel Moondoc and the late Glenn Spearman.

Malik is relatively unknown as a leader—most people know him for his work with Cecil Taylor in the mid- to late-1970s (on albums like *Dark To Themselves, The Cecil Taylor Unit* and *3 Phasis*). He's is a powerhouse trumpeter, whose upper-register runs can venture close to the pain threshold but who, at the same time, is capable of smooth bop-influenced groove-playing. This is particularly evident on the subtle, bluesy "Dominant Predicate," which opens his 1999 release *ConSequences*. On the disc, Malik is joined by saxophonist Sabir Mateen (best-known for his work with Test, but who also has two Eremite releases of his own—the trio date *Divine Mad Love* and *We Are Not At The Opera*, a duo with Sunny Murray), William Parker and the late drummer Denis Charles. Malik's other album for the label, 1997's *The Short Form*, features a different quartet—Spearman on tenor saxophone, George Langford on bass and Dennis Warren on drums—and is a more aggressive, blasting set of music.

Jemeel Moondoc, the alto saxophonist and composer who first brought the members of Other Dimensions In Music together in the 1970s (as his group Muntu), is another unfairly ignored figure. He's as strongly influenced by Ornette Coleman as any other post-1959 alto saxophonist (Coleman often seems to have stolen Charlie Parker's instrument away from him, in terms of influencing those to come), but he's also a dominating and exploratory spirit, going into corners even Ornette left dark. Moondoc cuts loose on the bandstand with thickly knotted streams of notes, often playing harshly but never offering anything that's not, in its own way, beautiful. He's released three CDs of material on Eremite: 1996's *Tri-P-Let*, 1997's *Fire In The Valley* and 1999's *New World Pygmies*, a series of duos with William Parker.

Though the duo format can seem a little sparse to some ears, on *New World Pygmies* it's anything but. Parker and Moondoc play with, at, and around each other, creating enough music for a half-dozen albums, in practically every style they know. Moondoc's playing is rough and his pacing is breath-based, like Peter Brötzmann's. The notes come out as gasping lungfuls, while Parker thrums and throbs underneath him, buoying his flights and always being ready to catch the saxophonist on the way back down. On the title track, Moondoc's notes pop like bubbles in the air, while Parker plays a dance-music that's not as much about keeping the listener's feet moving as it is about imagining *him* dancing while he plays. Other selections, like the ballad "Another Angel Goes Home," a Parker composition offered as a tribute to the late drummer Denis Charles, are beautiful in a coruscating way, the melody emerging like patterns of rust on a vast sheet of metal. *Fire In The Valley,* by contrast, is a 40-minute live workout, followed by a 90-second encore. Unlike a typical saxophone-trio rhythm section, bassist John Voigt and drummer Laurence Cook stay out of Jemeel's way for the most part, never really driving him forward. Instead, they create a tangential conversation and periodically check in with him. There are a few moments of collective action, when the whole trio rushes forward as one, but vast swaths of the piece are showcases for Moondoc as surely as if he'd been on the stage alone. The mere fact that it provides a platform for lesser-known musicians like Jemeel Moondoc is justification enough for Eremite's continued existence—the discs they've released by the late tenor saxophonist Glenn Spearman only cement Mike Ehlers' karmic standing.

Spearman, who died in 1998 of liver cancer at 50, was a ferocious player who didn't get as much notice as he should have during his lifetime, primarily because he lived and worked mostly in the Bay Area of northern California, not a real hotbed of avant-garde jazz. He released two CDs—*Mystery Project* and *Smokehouse*—on Black Saint, and three others on Cadence or CIMP (*Utterance, th,* and *Working With the Elements*). The influence of late-period Coltrane was always prominent in his music, though he clearly had his own voice, which had only begun to be documented at the time of his death. His two Eremite discs—*First And Last* and *Live At Fire In The Valley* (credited to Trio Hurricane)—have a fascinating immediacy. His notes and phrases are like hunks of raw meat, still bleeding as he slaps them down on the table in front of the listener. On the Trio Hurricane disc, he's joined by William Parker on bass and Paul Murphy on drums. The three play five pieces in just under an hour; some, like "N.Y.N.Y.," are herky-jerky, blues-based romps, while "Tones For William" is a long ballad, dense and resonant. Spearman screams and barks throughout the disc. It's not the music of a person with a year to live, not at all.

Nor is the music on *First And Last* that of someone almost literally on the brink of death. The disc documents, as the liner notes put it, "Glenn Spearman's last ever earth gig, performing or recording." He fronted a trio composed of himself, pianist Matthew Goodheart and Other Dimensions In Music drummer Rashid Bakr. The group plays two pieces, "Intertextual Reference" and "Under the Incalculable Sky, Listless, Diseased with Stars," each about 20 minutes long. Spearman is in full voice throughout, bellowing when he wants to, murmuring at other times, but never aiming for a note he's unable to reach. His disease never took away his voice until it stifled him for good. Goodheart and Bakr are solid enough accompanists. The pianist seems a little too eager to head into shimmering-waves-of-notes territory sometimes, without a real road map to get himself there or back, but there's never the sense of a guy on a tightrope, flailing his arms and knowing he better not stop as it's a long way to the ground if he does. Similarly, Bakr keeps the whole thing remarkably together; his work with Other Dimensions has prepared him admirably for maintaining a steady flow and implying interplay where there may not be as much unity-of-conception as there should be. In any case, the sheer historic importance of the session makes it a must. The music isn't perfect, but there will never be more, so everything that is present on *First And Last* takes on added resonance. It's Glenn Spearman's last gift to the world, and it's definitely worth keeping around.

The records released by Brooklyn's other free jazz label, No More Records, are as different from Eremite's catalog as Eremite's are from Aum Fidelity's. Alan Schneider owns No More, in addition to being Matthew Shipp's manager, and like Steven Joerg and Michael Ehlers, he has very specific ideas about the music and what he sees as his role in its dissemination and preservation. "A lot of the stuff I put out is small recordings, solo or duo recordings," Schneider told me. "I feel that those are the records in an artist's career that are seen as key records. Having a solo piano record by Matt Shipp or Anthony Braxton, or a William Parker/Joe Morris duo, or a Matt Shipp/Rob Brown duo, I feel those are key records. My focus is on the composer and improviser, focusing on the sonic techniques of the recording and putting out audiophile quality records. One of the first jobs I had was at an audiophile label, and I learned quite a bit about that style of recording. It's about trying to make definitive artistic statements with the artist, and not so much concentrating on putting out a hit record."

No More's releases are intimate documents, and it must be emphasized that the sound quality is often unbelievably beautiful. Not the kind of records to be put on and listened to with half an ear, they are for the most part deep-core drilling exercises, heading towards the very center of the performers' art. The most obstreperous items in the label's catalog are *Ancestral Homeland* (the second CD by Roy Campbell's Pyramid Trio), and *Jumping Off the Page* (by the Rob Brown Quartet). Far more typical are Matthew Shipp's *Symbol Systems* and William Parker's *Lifting The Sanctions,* both solo discs. The Shipp disc, recorded in 1995, contains 14 highly personal tracks that sport titles like "Self-Regulated Motion," "Nerve Signals" and "Algebraic Boogie." As might be surmised, it takes Shipp's obsessions with mathematics and cellular structure about as far as can be. For much of the record, Shipp fixates on specific patterns of notes, particularly at the low end of the keyboard's range, repeating them over and over and sounding more like Thelonious Monk than he has on almost any other disc in his catalog. In fact, *Symbol Systems* reveals itself most clearly, in all its intricacies, when played alongside Monk's *Thelonious Himself* album. Parker's solo album (his second; the first, Zero-In Records' *Testimony,* is out of print) features longer pieces than *Symbol Systems'* nuggets and shards of melody. Parker bows the bass, expanding the language of his music in ways not often heard even in his most radically extended pieces as a leader. Solo bass albums are not for everybody; few performers even attempt them. But *Lifting The Sanctions* is a record that anyone who's already been touched by William Parker's music should certainly seek out. It doesn't embrace the listener. It doesn't seem to be about communication nearly as much as it gives the sense of eavesdropping.

Schneider has a very keen sense of the market for free jazz, and the place his records have in it. "The problem with my discs is that they're not going to sell until well into the careers of the artists. They may not be the most appealing to the person that wants to hear a group, but for the real listener, that's where you get the real essence of a person. These are key records, but they're the least successful. The people who really listen to the music are gonna buy these records." He agrees that, among the three main independent labels, a complete—or nearly so—portrait of the New York players emerges. "I agree with Michael that clearly the best performances are the live performances, but there are lots of snafus that come with documenting the live performances. I stake a ground by putting out commercial records. I stand by that. Steven puts out more hit-oriented records, working with Other Dimensions In Music and David Ware and Little Huey—those are more album-oriented concepts, and that's Steve's background. He comes from a rock background. He opens doors for a lot of people, packaging the music that way."

Eremite, No More and Aum Fidelity are, of course, only the three longest-lived and best-known independent labels currently releasing free jazz. Others, like Chicago's Okka Disk and North Carolina's Wobbly Rail, have also released records by some of these players. Okka Disk sticks primarily to Chicago-based artists like saxophonists Fred Anderson and Ken Vandermark, but as a result of that, they've also become quite a showcase for drummer Hamid Drake. Drake plays behind Anderson on all his discs for the label, and is also part of Vandermark's DKV (Drake-Kessler-Vandermark) Trio, which recorded the *Deep Telling* CD with Joe Morris in 1999.

Recently, Matthew Shipp has gotten into the record-mogul game himself. Since 2000, he's been curating the Blue Series, released through Thirsty Ear. The series has four volumes so far—Shipp's *Pastoral Composure*, the William Parker Trio's *Painter's Spring*, Mat Maneri's *Blue Decco* and Shipp's *New Orbit*. Each of these records is a stripped-down gesture by the artists, more conventionally swinging than much of their past work (except for *New Orbit*, which abdicates swing for something entirely different, as discussed in Chapter Four). By providing a window into unexpected aspects of the artists' technique and vision, the Blue Series is rapidly becoming one of the most interesting projects in jazz. Upcoming releases include projects by alto saxophonist Tim Berne, pianist Craig Taborn and a new Roy Campbell quartet featuring vibraphonist Khan Jamal.

Another new label on the scene is Mat Maneri's Main Wave, intended primarily to issue music recorded by the violinist and his multi-instrumentalist father Joe. Scheduled for release in 2001 are *The Peace Concert*, a 1966 recording by Joe Maneri (tenor sax) and Pete Dolger (drums); *Painted Cottage Door*, which features Tom Halter (flugelhorn), Joe Maneri (piano), Mat Maneri (baritone violin), and John McLellen (drums); *Crazeology*, by the quintet of Joe McPhee (tenor sax), Mat Maneri (viola), Joe Maneri (piano), Ed Schuller (bass), and Randy Peterson (drums); *Going To Church*, with Joe Maneri (reeds), Roy Campbell (trumpet), Mat Maneri (viola), Matthew Shipp (piano), Barre Phillips (bass), and Randy Peterson (drums); and a session, untitled at this writing, featuring T.K. Ramakrishnan (mridangam), Mat Maneri (viola), and Chris Lightcap (bass). If, as Matthew Shipp has stated, Maneri represents "the future of the music," this label may prove to be a crucial source for new and exciting sounds as the years go on. But, all the labels discussed here are doing vitally important work. Every note of free jazz released by an indie label is a note that would never have been heard had its dissemination been left up to some corporate colossus.

• Hamid Drake

XIII • CREATING THE FUTURE

A few months after I began writing this book, I learned that the David S. Ware Quartet would be going into the studio to record their next album, *Corridors & Parallels,* before my manuscript was due. I decided on the spot that sitting in on the session would be the ideal concluding grace note for the book. I could talk about the evolution of the music, the interaction between bandmembers, and the creative process and since I'd opened with a description of a live performance by the quartet, the recording session seemed like the perfect bookend. Like most things, though, this turned out very differently than I'd originally imagined it would.

Two weeks before the quartet was to begin recording, they were totally unprepared, totally unrehearsed. This was deliberate. "We're going to improvise this record," Ware told me over the phone. "I want things to be totally fresh, and they will be in the sense that it's a new instrument and it's unrehearsed, so that's gonna provide the freshness. I'm not gonna write anything either."

The new instrument he was talking about was the Korg synthesizer he'd purchased. On the new album, *Corridors & Parallels,* which marks the quartet's return to Aum Fidelity after two releases on Columbia Jazz, Matthew Shipp doesn't play a note of piano. Instead, he improvises on the synthesizer, using programmed tone-structures he and Ware have chosen. "We're all master improvisers, so we can do this," Ware told me. "With our skills, and our sensitivity to one another, it'll be possible. It'll be fun, and it'll be interesting, cause we've never done it before. We're gonna call upon our spontaneous senses." Three months earlier, on November 9, the quartet had introduced the synth as part of their live sound during a pair of Knitting Factory shows. I wasn't there, but somebody sent me a tape in the mail. Based on what I heard, I was intrigued and optimistic, anticipating the changes the new instrument would bring to their music in the studio.

On February 26, Day One of the sessions, the streets were already nearly dark when I arrived, just before 7 PM, at the studio–Sorcerer Sound, on Mercer Street. Matthew Shipp, Steven Joerg, and session photographer Laurie Stalter were all hanging around outside, talking. We went up to the fifth floor together, in a rattling industrial elevator, accompanied by one of the studio's staff. Inside, David Ware was already sitting in his glass booth, saxophone on its stand, a few sheets of mostly blank paper the only notes for the session. He had a list of codes for setting the synthesizer, and nothing more. He looked cautiously pessimistic, but that's how he always looks. Nobody was concerned.

William Parker arrived next, lugging his massive bass out of the elevator and into the main recording room. Everyone began setting up. It was decided that Shipp would be in the room farthest back, physically separated from his bandmates. He wasn't miked–the Korg would be plugged directly into the mixing board, audible to the other bandmembers through their headphones, and to those of us observing the session through speakers. But Shipp would be able to see the other players through the glass. This way, his usual habit of locking eyes with Parker as they work wouldn't be disrupted.

The first major problem arose just before 8 PM. Drummer Guillermo Brown still hadn't arrived, let alone set up his kit. He'd been seen–Shipp ran into him on the street, and was told he was en route to get his drums and would be back shortly–but the clock was ticking, hourly charges were being accrued, and there was no sign of him. Brown finally showed up just after eight. He began assembling his drum kit and positioning a set of chimes and a large gong within arm's reach of his stool. Meanwhile, engineer Chris Flam (a short guy whose shoulder-length blue hair has strands of plastic braided into it) set up microphones. Miking the drums and getting the right sound was going to take quite a while, so William, David, Matt, and I relaxed in the lounge area and watched WWF wrestling. (Steven, who was paying for the session, was unable to relax due to the delays.) Laurie took pictures of the musicians as they sat patiently on the couches, but she had a tough time getting decent shots inside the studio proper, because of reflections off all the glass.

It was 9 PM before work began. The studio was only booked until midnight, and Steven was more than a little antsy when the quartet finally took their positions and began to play. Ware called out a code number, indicating the keyboard setting Matt should use and also providing a "working title" for the resultant piece.

The music was nothing like what I'd expected. Even after hearing the tape of the live set, I'd still assumed it would be strongly related to the music the quartet had always made, with maybe some Fender Rhodes-style electric piano/organ tones in place of a traditional piano. Something a little bluesier, a little funkier, than the blowouts Ware had dealt in to date, but still fairly grounded, and a logical next step from the group's last album, *Surrendered*. What actually happened was something I'd have never expected. Matt Shipp was playing long, droning tones on the keyboard—the shifts from one note to another were barely perceptible. It was more like a single, oscillating tone, rising and then falling again, than it was like any music I'd ever heard him play before. None of his typical staccato, key-pounding cellular structures were there, and the rhythm he usually offers was absent, too. I was immediately and strongly reminded of avant-garde classical composers like Alvin Lucier or LaMonte Young, or the soundtracks to mid-1980s films by director John Carpenter, like *Christine* and *Escape From New York*.

The second piece wasn't as shocking as the first; I was aware of Ware's method, and listened, fascinated, wondering what would emerge from this new sound. The song began in an even more soundtrack-like manner than its predecessor had. Shipp programmed the synth to create a tone like outer-space choirs. Parker's bass and

Brown's drums sculpted a skittering, throbbing pattern which, though complex, induced a great sense of calm throughout the studio and the booth. The music the trio was creating was like a jazz version of a piece by ambient-electronic titans the Orb. When Ware began playing, though, he seemed to come from a totally different place. It was like he wasn't listening to the other three at all. His solo was extremely free, sounding brilliant at times and other times like he was casting about in search of a melody, or just an idea solid enough to grab and ride for a significant stretch of time. The whole thing, as a chunk of sound, was disconcerting and disorienting. As though in response to Ware's soloing, Brown's drumming became more scattered, and far too busy to properly mate with Shipp's keyboards, which were rising and falling like the singers who heralded the arrival of the Starship Enterprise on old episodes of *Star Trek*. By the end of the piece, it had transformed itself from a delicate ballad to a fight between Ware's obstreperous ranting—with Brown scuffling around behind him—and Shipp's clouds of ethereal singers. It was the single weirdest thing I'd ever heard the Ware quartet perform, and the session had barely begun.

It was getting on towards 11 PM when I left the studio for the night. The group had come into the booth to listen to the first piece, and one-and-a-half takes of the second. They were planning on going right back to recording after they'd checked their results thus far, but—as ever—I was at the mercy of NJ Transit, so I made a run for it. On the ride home, I thought about what I'd been hearing, and what I'd seen, thus far.

I'd also observed for a few hours during the recording of *Surrendered*. I remembered sitting in the booth watching and listening as the band recorded two versions of "Peace Celestial," one of which eventually opened the CD. They also laid down a radical deconstruction of the Beatles' "Yesterday" while I was there, but that cut remains unreleased. It wasn't just the contrast between the smooth, composed music of *Surrendered* and the scrabbling, on-the-fly stuff played only hours before that was sticking in my head, though it was the whole mood of the session. The *Surrendered* session seemed like everything a jazz recording date should be. Everyone knew what was expected of them going in, and beautiful music was created from a shared conception of the sonic goal and the strengths of the ensemble. What I'd seen at Sorcerer Sound couldn't have been further away from that. From the late start, to the conflicting musical directions, the whole endeavor felt chaotic to me. And it didn't feel like the kind of roiling, spirit-shaking chaos that can bring out the best in free jazz musicians. It felt like nobody knew where the whole thing was supposed to go, and they were just continuing to play to see if a clue would fall out of the air and show them the finish-line.

When they were in the booth listening, as I made my way out, their faces were neutral. They weren't looking around to see what their bandmates thought; each musician was lost in his own world, concentrating on the sound and (it seemed to me) trying to pick something of value out of the morass. I realized, as I walked through the darkened streets from the train station to my apartment, that for the first time since I'd known these musicians, I was worried that they might fail in what they were attempting – and worse, I wasn't totally convinced anybody there (Steven Joerg, David Ware, or anybody else in the group) even knew what it was they were trying to do.

I was late getting to the studio the following morning, as I had an interview further downtown which started at the same time the session did. But when I finally walked in, the quartet was in the middle of a piece, and from the first notes I heard, something was different. Steven was smiling; so was Chris Flam. The bandmembers, behind the glass, were playing their instruments with a greater looseness and a joy that came through the speakers and even the air.

The piece they were working on was sparse, yet filled with a desolate romanticism, like Japanese music. Shipp's keyboard tones were far away from the washes he was essaying the night before; he was splashing individual notes down like liquid mercury. The keyboard sounded like a koto; like neon reflecting in puddles beside a midnight sidewalk. Guillermo Brown was barely touching his drums, concentrating instead on the chimes, occasionally swishing a brush over the cymbals and accenting the suspenseful, floating-in-air mood of his thoughts with taps on the large, hanging gong, or an isolated thump from the bass pedal. William was droning, bowing the bass at the lower edge of its range almost like he was trying to fill in the bottom spaces left open by Guillermo's drifting, meditative playing. David was immeasurably more attuned to the rest of the group than he'd been the previous night—he was blowing long tones, using circular breathing to suspend notes past the point at which most people would pass out on the floor. The humming vibrations he was creating went almost imperceptibly up and down, mesmerizing me as I listened. Finally, after nearly four minutes of whistling drones, he erupted into a perfectly timed, reverb-soaked, scrabbling solo as Shipp continued to drip metallic, gleaming notes behind him. When the piece ended, I was overjoyed. This was nothing that I could have anticipated, based on the live tape or the previous night's abortive efforts. This was as beautiful as anything the quartet had ever recorded, but utterly unlike anything they'd ever played, or anything I'd ever heard.

There was a break for lunch. Everyone gathered in the main room to eat except David, who headed for the back room, to seek out additional inspiration from the keyboard's banks of pre-programmed sounds. Conversation was upbeat; everyone was happy with the way things were going. I talked to Guillermo about electronic music, and Matt about mainstream jazz players and their overinflated reputations. There was laughter and joking; nobody talked about the chaos of the night before—it had been forgotten in the rush of productivity that'd come with the new day.

What happened next, musically speaking, was just weird. David decided to investigate the rhythmic possibilities of his new machine. The next sound to boom out of the control-booth speakers was a hilariously obvious, almost generic hip-hop beat. Matt Shipp hit a few notes on the keyboard and began emitting a thick electric-piano sound that was the purest evocation of early 1980s funk I'd heard since high school. He began riffing on the sound, against the beat, and David catapulted into a wild, almost out-of-control solo, the harshest and most unhinged thing he'd played thus far. William and Guillermo filled in exactly what was required, rhythmically, the drummer doing little more than punctuating the primary, machine-generated rhythm. The track was downright bizarre; totally unexpected, it sounded like *Future Shock*-era Herbie Hancock remixing circa-1966 Pharaoh Sanders. Even as it was happening, I could tell from Steven Joerg's reaction that it wasn't gonna make the album. Still, it was so exhilarating to hear the band play this kind of fat groove that it seemed like just the thing to launch the quartet back into a music-creating mood after lunch.

The next track to be recorded was the only piece of music from the entire session which wasn't cut live and left alone. Another rhythm-based workout, it was initially built around Shipp's keyboards and Ware's saxophone, with no contribution at all from Parker or Brown. The synth was programmed to sound like a Latin percussionist gone berserk–there was a steady trap-drum sequence, and various keys provided sonic accents. Whistles, conga drums and other salsa-esque devices emerged from the machine as Ware tore into another wild, unfettered solo. Listening back to the track, though, David decided Guillermo should overdub additional percussion. The drummer headed into the recording room, and the track poured out of the speakers again. The exercise went afield almost immediately. Ware was expecting Brown to add a steady drum track to the piece, thus bringing his saxophone playing into sharper relief. Instead, Guillermo blasted through a berserk, almost rock-like drum solo, turning Shipp's keyboard into the foundation for an *Interstellar Space*-like drums-and-saxophone duel. The instant recording was complete on the track, Ware's displeasure, though not vocalized, was quite clear. The piece was abandoned with no comment, and the quartet moved on to other things. I kept my opinion–that it was one of the best, most forceful things to come out of the session so far–to myself.

I stayed long enough to witness the creation of two more pieces. The first was a little schizophrenic. Matt Shipp returned to the swooshing keyboard sounds of the first night's recording, and this time it seemed to distance him from the rest of the ensemble. William and Guillermo, who'd been assuming relatively minor roles throughout a lot of the session (or at least not making their usual extroverted contributions to the group sound) locked in with David this time. The result was an impressive saxophone-trio track, with a keyboard hissing and floating somewhere around the margins; an interesting reversal of the power dynamic that had been in place to that point.

On the last piece I heard them record, Shipp turned the keyboard into a pipe organ. The clearly liturgical overtones of the keyboard brought complementary performances out of Parker and Ware. The bassist, in particular, seemed to be going for a religious experience on his instrument–he was strumming the strings like it was a massive guitar, creating throbbing waves of sound that seemed to shake the Plexiglas panels separating the various recording booths. Brown, meanwhile, attacked his drums in as forceful a manner as he'd done thus far, taking off on an over-the-top, Art-Blakey-esque series of hard-bop assault-riffs. David kept pace with his backing musicians quite ably, and the whole quartet came together in the creation of something really impressive. When it wound down, though, I looked at my watch and realized I had to leave before everything was complete (again). Without saying anything to disturb the musicians, I waved a quick goodbye to everybody in the mixing room and jumped in the elevator down to the street.

I was feeling much better about the album as I headed home the second time. Not all of what I'd heard was brilliant, and not all of it deserved to be released, but the diamonds outnumbered the lumps of coal by a significant margin. It was going to be a good record, and more than that, it was going to surprise everyone who hears it, was my feeling. That element of total sonic surprise hasn't always been present on Ware's albums.

When I spoke to Matt Shipp two days later, his feelings were close to my own. "For me it was fun," he said. "I'm always looking for new challenges, and definitely have my pianistic personality out there as far as records are concerned. There's ample material for people out there, so this was just something different and therefore fun. I completely went into the session for what this session is." He and I agreed that things got off to a somewhat rocky start; he admitted he "would have run the session differently than it was run." Nevertheless, "I think a lot of really good stuff came out of it, that can make for an intriguing album."

I waited a few more days before calling David Ware for his thoughts. Finally, a full week after the sessions, we got on the phone. He, too, was happy with the results, but as always was cautious and reserved about his comments. "We got the music but...the session was a little strained," he told me. I didn't mention my own mild panic on the first night. "It wasn't the easiest session I've had, for a couple of reasons. One, we were working with all new people. The engineer, it was the first time working with this band." Matt Shipp had recorded at Sorcerer Sound in the past, but Ware never had. "There seemed to be some technical problems every now and then." This, too, was true—at a few points, particularly during the second day, programmed sequences selected by David or Matthew seemed to throw off the system and cause the booth computer to fail to record the synth. "And then there was the fact that there was no rehearsal, so I didn't pre-think-out anything. And I did that on purpose; I wanted to do something different. So that was a factor in it also." Still, Ware didn't seem to regret any of the decisions he made going into the session. "Listening back, I think that it worked out well. Not everything worked, but most of it did. I think I was able to come up with a variety of pieces as though it had been rehearsed. So overall, I think we got what we needed, but it wasn't easy to get. I felt that it was not without a great amount of effort. Probably the most difficult session that I can think of."

I asked Ware about the track that was sticking out in my mind most clearly, the piece onto which Guillermo Brown overdubbed a drum solo after-the-fact. I had the feeling I knew what he was going to say before he said it, and I was proved correct. "That doesn't work for me," he said. "We're not gonna use that. In the beginning of that, I said let's try Guillermo, Matt and myself, and listening to that I thought it would make the music too complicated. I wanted to play a piece with me and steady rhythm. I didn't want the rhythm to change. I wanted a steady rhythm throughout. To superimpose Guillermo on top of that, it was too much. It made it more complex than I wanted. I wanted to be able to manage what I was playing, without having to think about someone else's superimposition. I just wanted one juxtaposition to that rhythm: myself. That's why there was no bass, that's why I said let's do it with just Matthew. So I think that original track worked out fine. But the superimposition didn't work." Still, Ware is looking forward to working with electronics more in the future. "We're gonna use piano and keyboard for the live shows," he told me. "We've got two tours coming up, and I'm planning on using both for both tours." There's going to be some ex post facto tweaking done to the raw material, between recording and release, but Ware said "there's not that much that has to be done. There's a few things...but not much. Basically, [the tracks are] gonna be as is. It's just a matter of finding the right order."

Hanging up the phone, I thought about my own impressions of the music that Ware was creating on this disc, and what it meant for the future of his music, and free jazz as a whole. I surprised myself by coming to the conclusion that it doesn't "mean" all that much. Avant-garde musicians have been incorporating electronic sounds since Sun Ra's recordings with primitive synthesizers in the 1950s. Merely inserting electronics doesn't fundamentally change the music. Only when programmed rhythms take away the organic interaction that's at the heart of improvisation does jazz suffer. And as Ware himself told me prior to the recording, "Try to look at it from my perspective. We've got 12 or 13 albums out there with the quartet. It's time for a different sound. It makes good sense to have some variety. It's time for a change is all." The music of the David S. Ware Quartet, whatever the instrumentation, will continue to be the product of the four people behind those instruments. Therefore, the relationship they've cultivated–as musicians, friends and kindred spirits–will continue to shine through the musical notes. This is not like Sonny Rollins bringing in an entirely new backing band to record a disco fusion album (as he did in the 1970s). This is the avant-garde going in a direction that, frankly, nobody else is heading right now. Most jazz players, confronted with a synthesizer or wishing to interact with one, would wind up wallowing in wan funk riffs or oozing melted-butter ballads with phony strings rising up behind them like a greeting-card photo of a sunset. Ware and his quartet have, instead, transformed their music into something wholly new. At points, it's as harsh as anything they've ever recorded, but in many ways it's like a science fiction version of free jazz.

When I first conceived of this chapter, I thought it would impose some kind of structure, create a master narrative. I don't even think that's a good idea anymore (it cuts a little too close to the "great man theory" I was criticizing in Chapter Eleven), and I certainly don't think it's happened. I began this story in the middle, and I'm ending it just a little farther down the road. Free jazz existed before me, and it will continue to exist not only after this book is published, but for decades to come, as far as I can tell. It's extraordinarily healthy right now, and its audience is growing–slowly, but steadily.

All I can really offer, by way of a conclusion, is this: the avant-garde is forever talking about taking the music forward. This record may not take the whole of free jazz forward, as a lot of bands won't be inclined to put their own spin on the ideas David Ware and his compatriots are working with now. This isn't a sign of cowardice, but of the diverse musical paths the players and groups I've tried to document in these pages have chosen to take. But this album is a sign that these four players are heading forward, and they're not looking back to see if anyone else is following. They're just doing it because, as John Lee Hooker said so many years ago, it's in them, and it's got to come out. And that's been the reason every great piece of music has entered the world, from the beginning of time.

As I write these final pages, every musician I've profiled here has recording sessions lined up, shows booked, and albums in the can awaiting release. Sabir Mateen of Test has a duo album with Hamid Drake ready to drop on Eremite. Cecil Taylor, William Parker and Tony Oxley recently recorded a 10-CD box, documenting a week's worth of shows at Ronnie Scott's jazz club in London. Roy Campbell is going into the studio with vibraphonist Khan Jamal, for a volume in Thirsty Ear's Blue Series. And on and on. The music doesn't stop—it couldn't be covered, even in a book much longer than this one, without the text being incomplete or out of date by the time the first copy came back from the printer. I hope this book serves the purpose for which I wrote it: to introduce, to a new and open-minded audience, the musicians I feel are creating the most vital jazz music of today, and tomorrow as well. Now it's up to you, the reader, to do the rest of the legwork on your own. There will always be more records, more performances, more music. Enjoy it all.

APPENDIX I : RECOMMENDED LISTENING

The following is a list of recommended free jazz records. Some have been extensively discussed in the preceding pages; some have been mentioned in passing; others have not been mentioned at all. Still, taken together, they represent a significant portion of the output of the musicians profiled in this book, and as such they also represent some of the best new jazz music being made, anywhere in the world.

Some of these records are decades old, and are regarded as "classics" of free jazz; others (the majority) have been released in the last ten years. All of them are vital, compelling works of art which will provide not only an immediate, visceral thrill, but literally years of pleasure as you come back to them again and again, plumbing their depths and catching all the stuff you missed the last time you put one of them on.

This is, of course, an incomplete list. Many of these players have other records, some of which skulked into stores years ago on vinyl and never made the transition to CD, or appeared on CD on some tiny label that vanished after printing 1000 copies and getting ripped off by distributors, and others that I didn't feel represented their work well. There are probably a lot more that I just didn't know about. When contemplating the headlong dive into accumulation that this list represents, remember that the record business is a business after all, and art goes by the wayside 99 times out of a hundred. Many of these releases may not be long for store shelves. So grab them when and where you see them, and hopefully you will find that they are not only pleasurable in and of themselves, but are the springboard to a lifetime of record collecting and appreciation for free jazz as a living, fiery, ever-changing music with the power to alter every sensory perception.

FRED ANDERSON QUARTET—*The Milwaukee Tapes, Vol. 1* (Atavistic)
FRED ANDERSON TRIO—*Live At The Velvet Lounge* (Okka Disk)
FRED ANDERSON—*Fred Anderson/DKV Trio* (Okka Disk)
FRED ANDERSON, HAMID DRAKE, KIDD JORDAN, WILLIAM PARKER—
   Two Days In April (Eremite)
ART ENSEMBLE OF CHICAGO—*Live* (Delmark)
ART ENSEMBLE OF CHICAGO—*Bap-Tizum* (Koch)
ART ENSEMBLE OF CHICAGO—*Fanfare For The Warriors* (Koch)
ART ENSEMBLE OF CHICAGO—*Urban Bushmen* (ECM)
ALBERT AYLER TRIO—*Spiritual Unity* (ESP-Disk)
PETER BROTZMANN SEXTET & QUARTET—*Nipples* (Atavistic)
PETER BROTZMANN—*Machine Gun* (FMP)
PETER BROTZMANN—*Die Like A Dog* (FMP)
ROB BROWN—*Breath Rhyme* (Silkheart)
ROB BROWN—*Youniverse* (Riti)
ROB BROWN/MATTHEW SHIPP—*Blink Of An Eye* (No More)
ROB BROWN—*Scratching The Surface* (CIMP)
ROB BROWN QUARTET—*Jumping Off The Page* (No More)
TOM BRUNO/SABIR MATEEN—*Getting Away With Murder* (Eremite)
ROY CAMPBELL—*New Kingdom* (Delmark)
ROY CAMPBELL PYRAMID—*Communion* (Silkheart)
ROY CAMPBELL PYRAMID TRIO—*Ancestral Homeland* (No More)
ROY CAMPBELL—*Ethnic Stew & Brew* (Delmark)
ORNETTE COLEMAN—*The Shape Of Jazz To Come* (Atlantic)
ORNETTE COLEMAN—*This Is Our Music* (Atlantic)
ORNETTE COLEMAN—*Free Jazz* (Atlantic)
JOHN COLTRANE—*Ascension* (Impulse!)
JOHN COLTRANE—*Meditations* (Impulse!)
JOHN COLTRANE—*Interstellar Space* (Impulse!)
JOHN COLTRANE—*Live In Japan* (GRP/Impulse!)
ANDREW CYRILLE—*Metamusicians' Stomp* (Black Saint)
WHIT DICKEY TRIO—*Transonic* (Aum Fidelity)
WHIT DICKEY QUARTET—*Big Top* (Wobbly Rail)
DIE LIKE A DOG QUARTET—*Little Birds Have Fast Hearts, Vol. 1* (FMP)
DIE LIKE A DOG QUARTET—*Little Birds Have Fast Hearts, Vol. 2* (FMP)

DIE LIKE A DOG QUARTET—*From Valley To Valley* (Eremite)
ARTHUR DOYLE/SUNNY MURRAY—*Dawn Of A New Vibration* (Fractal)
CHARLES GAYLE/WILLIAM PARKER/RASHIED ALI—
   Touchin' On Trane (FMP)
CHARLES GAYLE—*Kingdom Come* (Knitting Factory)
CHARLES GAYLE—*Homeless* (Silkheart)
CHARLES GAYLE—*Spirits Before* (Silkheart)
CHARLES GAYLE—*Ancient Of Days* (Knitting Factory)
CHARLES GAYLE—*Repent* (Knitting Factory)
RAPHE MALIK—*The Short Form* (Eremite)
RAPHE MALIK—*ConSequences* (Eremite)
JOE MANERI/MAT MANERI—*Blessed* (ECM)
JOE MANERI/MAT MANERI/JOE MORRIS—*Three Men Walking* (ECM)
MAT MANERI QUARTET—*Blue Decco* (Thirsty Ear)
MAT MANERI—*Trinity* (ECM)
JOE McPHEE—*Nation Time* (Atavistic)
JOE McPHEE—*Trinity* (Atavistic)
JOE McPHEE/HAMID DRAKE—*Emancipation Proclamation,*
   a Real Statement of Freedom (Okka Disk)
MAT MANERI TRIO— *Fever Bed* (Leo)
JEMEEL MOONDOC TRIO—*Tri-P-Let* (Eremite)
JEMEEL MOONDOC TRIO—*Fire In The Valley* (Eremite)
JEMEEL MOONDOC/WILLIAM PARKER—*New World Pygmies* (Eremite)
JOE MORRIS—*Singularity* (Aum Fidelity)
JOE MORRIS—*Sweatshop* (Riti)
JOE MORRIS TRIO—*Flip & Spike* (Riti)
JOE MORRIS ENSEMBLE—*Elsewhere* (Homestead)
JOE MORRIS/WILLIAM PARKER—*Invisible Weave* (No More)
JOE MORRIS TRIO—*Antennae* (Aum Fidelity)
JOE MORRIS/DKV TRIO—*Deep Telling* (Okka Disk)
JOE MORRIS QUARTET—*You Be Me* (Soul Note)
JOE MORRIS QUARTET—*A Cloud Of Black Birds* (Aum Fidelity)
JOE MORRIS QUARTET—*Underthru* (Soul Note)
JOE MORRIS QUARTET—*At The Old Office* (Knitting Factory)
JOE MORRIS/MAT MANERI—*Soul Search* (Aum Fidelity)
SONNY MURRAY—*Sonny's Time Now* (DIW)
SUNNY MURRAY/SABIR MATEEN—*We Are Not At The Opera* (Eremite)
SUNNY MURRAY/CHARLES GAYLE—*Illuminators* (Audible Hiss)
OTHER DIMENSIONS IN MUSIC—*Other Dimensions In Music* (Silkheart)
OTHER DIMENSIONS IN MUSIC—*Now!* (Aum Fidelity)

OTHER DIMENSIONS IN MUSIC w/MATTHEW SHIPP—
 Time Is Of The Essence; The Essence Is Beyond Time (Aum Fidelity)
WILLIAM PARKER—*Through Acceptance Of The Mystery Peace* (Eremite)
WILLIAM PARKER'S LITTLE HUEY CREATIVE MUSIC ORCHESTRA—
 Flowers Grow In My Room (Centering)
WILLIAM PARKER—*Lifting The Sanctions* (No More)
WILLIAM PARKER'S IN ORDER TO SURVIVE—
 Compassion Seizes Bed-Stuy (Homestead)
WILLIAM PARKER'S LITTLE HUEY CREATIVE MUSIC ORCHESTRA—
 Sunrise In The Tone World (Aum Fidelity)
WILLIAM PARKER'S IN ORDER TO SURVIVE—
 The Peach Orchard (Aum Fidelity)
WILLIAM PARKER'S IN ORDER TO SURVIVE—*Posium Pendasem* (FMP)
WILLIAM PARKER'S LITTLE HUEY CREATIVE MUSIC ORCHESTRA—
 Mayor Of Punkville (Aum Fidelity)
WILLIAM PARKER TRIO—*Painter's Spring* (Thirsty Ear)
WILLIAM PARKER/HAMID DRAKE—*Piercing The Veil* (Aum Fidelity)
WILLIAM PARKER QUARTET—*O'Neal's Porch* (Centering)
IVO PERELMAN—*Cama de Terra* (Homestead)
IVO PERELMAN—*Sad Life* (Leo)
DEWEY REDMAN/CECIL TAYLOR/ELVIN JONES—
 Momentum Space (Verve)
SONNY SHARROCK—*Ask The Ages* (Axiom)
MATTHEW SHIPP/ROB BROWN—*Sonic Explorations* (Cadence)
MATTHEW SHIPP QUARTET—*Points* (Silkheart)
MATTHEW SHIPP TRIO—*Circular Temple* (Infinite Zero)
MATTHEW SHIPP DUO WITH WILLIAM PARKER—*Zo* (Infinite Zero)
MATTHEW SHIPP DUO WITH ROSCOE MITCHELL—*2-Z* (2.13.61)
MATTHEW SHIPP—*Symbol Systems* (No More)
MATTHEW SHIPP TRIO—*Prism* (hat Art)
MATTHEW SHIPP/MAT MANERI—*Gravitational Systems* (hat Art)
MATTHEW SHIPP TRIO—*By the Law Of Music* (hat Art)
MATTHEW SHIPP QUARTET—*Flow Of X* (2.13.61)
MATTHEW SHIPP QUARTET—*Critical Mass* (2.13.61)
MATTHEW SHIPP DUO WITH JOE MORRIS—*Thesis* (hat Art)
MATTHEW SHIPP HORN QUARTET—*Strata* (hat Art)
MATTHEW SHIPP TRIO—*The Multiplication Table* (hat Art)
MATTHEW SHIPP—*Before The World* (FMP)
MATTHEW SHIPP DUO WITH WILLIAM PARKER—*DNA* (Thirsty Ear)

MATTHEW SHIPP/ROB BROWN/WILLIAM PARKER—
Magnetism (Bleu Regard)

MATTHEW SHIPP QUARTET—*Pastoral Composure* (Thirsty Ear)

MATTHEW SHIPP—*New Orbit* (Thirsty Ear)

GLENN SPEARMAN—*First And Last* (Eremite)

CECIL TAYLOR—*Air Above Mountains* (Enja)

CECIL TAYLOR—*Nefertiti, The Beautiful One Has Come* (Revenant)

CECIL TAYLOR—*Dark To Themselves* (Enja)

CECIL TAYLOR—*The Cecil Taylor Unit* (New World)

CECIL TAYLOR—*3 Phasis* (New World)

CECIL TAYLOR—*Olu Iwa* (Soul Note)

TEST—*Live/Test* (Eremite)

TEST—*Test* (Ecstatic Peace)

TEST—*Test* (Aum Fidelity)

TRIO HURRICANE—*Live At Fire In The Valley* (Eremite)

DAVID S. WARE—*Passage To Music* (Silkheart)

DAVID S. WARE—*Great Bliss, Vol. 1* (Silkheart)

DAVID S. WARE—*Great Bliss, Vol. 2* (Silkheart)

DAVID S. WARE—*Flight Of I* (DIW/Columbia)

DAVID S. WARE—*Third Ear Recitation* (DIW)

DAVID S. WARE QUARTET—*Cryptology* (Homestead)

DAVID S. WARE QUARTET—*Dao* (Homestead)

DAVID S. WARE QUARTET—*Oblations And Blessings* (Silkheart)

DAVID S. WARE—*Earthquation* (DIW)

DAVID S. WARE—*Godspelized* (DIW)

DAVID S. WARE QUARTET—*Wisdom Of Uncertainty* (Aum Fidelity)

DAVID S. WARE—*Go See The World* (Columbia)

DAVID S. WARE—*Surrendered* (Columbia)

DAVID S. WARE—*Live In The Netherlands*
(Solo at Zuid-Nederlands Jazz Festival 1997) (Splasc(h))

DAVID S. WARE QUARTET—*Corridors &Parallels* (Aum Fidelity)

VARIOUS ARTISTS—*Wildflowers:*
The New York Loft Jazz Sessions (Knit Classics)

APPENDIX II : CONTACTS

The following is a short and, again, incomplete list of a dozen contacts that will get you well on your way to accumulating more free jazz records than you could ever listen to in your lifetime. Most of the addresses below are record labels; two are that, and more. Cadence puts out a monthly magazine covering jazz in all its aspects, and also runs two labels: Cadence Jazz and CIMP (the Cadence Improvised Music Project). This is explained in much more detail on their website. Forced Exposure releases a few records of their own, but mostly they're an incredible mail-order distributor. Investigating any and all of these places will inevitably lead you to others: happy hunting!

Atavistic Records
PO Box 578266
Chicago, IL 60657
www.atavistic.com

Aum Fidelity Records
PO Box 170147
Brooklyn, NY 11217
www.aumfidelity.com

Cadence
Cadence Building
Redwood, NY 13679
www.cadencemagazine.com

Eremite Records
PO Box 812
Northampton, MA 01061
www.eremite.com

Forced Exposure
226 Lowell Street
Somerville, MA 02144
www.forcedexposure.com

FMP/Free Music Production
Postbox 100 227
D-10562 Berlin Germany

Knitting Factory Records
74 Leonard Street
New York, NY 10013
www.knittingfactory.com

No More Records
PO Box 334
Woodmere, NY 11598

Okka Disk
PO Box 146472
Chicago, IL 60614-6472
www.okkadisk.com

Riti Records
7 Broadway Terrace
Cambridge, MA 02139

Silkheart Records
c/o Gazell Productions
PO Box 527
Mansfield Center, CT 06250

Wobbly Rail
PO Box 16206
Chapel Hill, NC 27516
wobbly.home.mindspring.com

ABOUT THE AUTHOR

Phil Freeman has been a freelance music critic since 1995, writing for newspapers and magazines such as the *Aquarian Weekly, Alternative Press, Magnet, Jazziz, Down Beat, Juggernaut,* and *Metal Hammer.* He is passionate about avant-garde jazz, but loves hardcore and death-metal as well, and writes about all of them with equal understanding and affection. His profiles of David S. Ware and Matthew Shipp in *Juggernaut* magazine were among the first articles to bridge the gap between the free jazz and extreme metal communities. This is his first book.